ALIENS ABOUT HUMANS

The Undercover Alien's Handbook on Successful Infiltration

Michael Sender

 Redford Wilkins Publishing

Copyright © 2024 by Michael Sender

ISBN: 978-91-531-0395-0 (print), ISBN 978-91-531-0396-7 (ebook)

For all of those who don't fit in.

Contents

By Aliens, For Aliens

I f you are reading this, you are likely an alien infiltrator on your way to Earth, assigned to collect intelligence and conduct covert operations while working undercover as a human. If so – brace yourself and read on carefully. You will need all the help you can get. Should you, by some terrible misfortune, happen to be human – be warned that what comes next may be hazardously disruptive to your worldview. The human psyche is highly unfit for perspectives on humanity that aren't biased by human cultural and ethical codes and may perceive them as insensitive and offensive (the meaning of these two exclusively human adjectives will be properly explained further ahead in the book). Human reader discretion is therefore strongly advised. If you identify as a human – destroy this book – and ideally yourself – immediately.

The few sentient creatures who have ever heard of the planet Earth know this tiny Solar satellite to be commonly associated with the deep ocean octopods, best known for their ink cloud party tricks which have ruined every galactic oxygen cocktail party terrestrials have ever been invited to. Yet, while most of Earth has been somewhat explored by certain segments of inter-stellar wormhole tourists, many of whom find this sombre oceanic world a relaxing and inexpensive escape from the shallow and starlit waters of their home planets, few know that almost twenty-nine percent of Earth's surface is actually covered by dry land and infested with some of the slowest creatures in the universe. The movement and deliberation speed of these creatures is so slow that almost any extraterres-trial can move past them at their natural pace without even being noticed. Some of these species are believed to be sentient and even somewhat intelligent. Humans are not one of them.

The intellectual capacity of a human is mediocre at best. Considered generally unremarkable compared to other galactic parasites, the human species is so rarely mentioned in mainstream literature that only a few unhealthily curious creatures living in the vicinity of the Solar system are properly aware of its existence. (The term "properly aware" reflects the ability to distin-guish this species from all the varieties of the Mercu-rian mud-vomiting tripod mantis.) However, humans do possess a level of ingenuity that allows them to develop technologies which, when wielded by similarly primitive beings, are capable of destroying planets and greatly depreciating galactic shareholder value.

When this inconvenient circumstance was first established, the interstellar scientific community quickly reached the consensus that the human infestation of the Solar system and its adjacent systems needed to be resolutely addressed. The initial extermination plan was voted down by the Galactic Council thanks to the immense efforts of the cat lobby, who have long amassed the greatest terrestrial influence over galactic affairs since the velociraptors died out, persistently stressing the importance of humans as their primary source of food and cardboard boxes. The plea was unexpectedly supported by the mouse lobby, who argued that the removal of humans from the value chain may create an imbalance in the terrestrial ecosystem which would likely put mice at a great disadvantage.

In the council's finally adopted resolution regarding the human threat, the word "eliminated" was replaced with "contained", upon which the problem was funnelled down to the Galactic Intelligence Service, from where it frequently boomeranged back to the dedicated Humanology faculty of the Galactic Academy of Sciences due to lack of intelligence.

It wasn't until the Human Infiltration Programme was initiated some millennia ago by the recently reinstalled Galactic Operations Department that we were able to acquire any meaningful insights into human life. The programme's objective was to gather intelligence on humans by allowing our operatives to assume human form and embed themselves in human societies, where they would live among humans and report their findings until their student debt was paid off or for as long as their mental health allowed.

The programme's primary objective was to monitor humanity and interfere just enough to keep humans contained on their home planet and away from anything else they could break. It was pioneered by the legendary infiltrator Zorn, whose chronicles still make up the larger bulk of our knowledge on humans. Zorn has conducted numerous infiltration missions on Earth. So many, in fact, that some of his most envious critics sometimes descend to making preposterous insinuations that he may have liked it there. Each mission was a greater adventure than the last. And yet none of Zorn's missions provided more practical insight into the peculiarities of humanity than the mission that followed Zorn's sudden disappearance. When the legendary infiltrator's contact with the mothership suddenly ceased, a search party was immediately dispatched to his last known location on Earth. The two agents assigned to locate Zorn, operatives Gee and Balbooza, had to go undercover as humans themselves in order to proceed with the search uncompromised. It was during this mission that the necessity for a proper instruction manual for aliens working undercover as humans became abundantly clear. The publishing of this handbook was a direct response to this dire need.

Every seasoned infiltrator will concur that human

infiltration is an extremely perilous task, given how little is still known about this species and how little sense most of its behaviour still makes to intelligent life-forms. The things you are about to experience will give you hellish nightmares for centuries to come. You may get psychologically maimed for life. You may also die. Not that there is anything on Earth that can seriously physically harm you, since you are most likely an ethereal creature that doesn't have a physical body. But you may end up *wanting* to die as a result of the prolonged embarrassment working undercover as a human inevitably entails.

Whether you think you deserve this punishing chore or not, may you find comfort in the fact that you are holding within your energy field of ionic receptors the most exhaustive source of knowledge about humans in the galaxy. Thousands of high-profile galactic scholars have worked hard on assembling any available knowledge about humans in this hands-on format, designed to aid our brave infiltrators in getting through the day. In addition, excerpts from Zorn's search party dialogues, which were transmitted back to the mothership for maximum transparency and to ensure the agents' access to timely psychological counsel, should provide some practical examples of how *not* to act when going undercover as humans. The excerpts also shed some light on the much speculated upon mystery of Zorn's disappearance.

With this said, good luck on your mission and do not abort unless you have read the whole manual and are still panicking. The mission's purpose and methods will be explained thoroughly throughout the handbook's nine chapters. Whenever the weight of your quest becomes completely unbearable, remember that you could have been sanitising the rot-covered crevices of the dead-born mind-reading glue slug farms of Khazur-Moomchah. If that doesn't help – just consider the fact that instead of wearing the body of this foul and embarrassing creature, you could have been hovering in a comfortable magnetic cloud with a nice view over Saturn's asteroid belt, sipping at the iconic ethereal coffee vapour of the Titanian Solar Observatory – had you taken your university studies a bit more seriously.

This may not help you either, but at least it is true.

Chapter 1

The Basics of Terrestrial Life

Before embarking on your infiltration mission, it is worth learning one or two things about this strange planet that has the sort of chemistry capable of spawning life forms as annoying as humans.

Earth is an oceanic world, partially scarred by human-infested land. Eighty-eight percent of the planet's surface is (mostly) safe from humans (either thanks to water or to poor mobile reception), with occasional minor infestation outbreaks known as "expeditions" and "cruises". The exact etymology of the planet's name so far remains unknown, but presumably the word "earth" originates from the sound a human makes when tasting it. Humans insist on referring to their planet as "*the* Earth" – a habit stemming from the fact that it is the only one of all the planets they have ever colonised (and unimaginatively named "Earth") that still has any organic life left on it. A more intelligent species might have seen this as a learning opportunity, but unfortunately the human lifespan is too short for them to learn anything substantially useful or to have to suffer the consequences of their impact on the planetary environment.

Earth is composed of a variety of chemicals and materials, very few of which humans haven't tried to smoke or extract alcohol from. Most chemicals are rather harmless, although humans are steadily adding new toxic ones. Presently, Earth's climate is too cold for our species to settle in, but the current level of carbon dioxide emissions from its fauna is likely to make this planet perfectly colonisable within less than two centuries, provided that we can prevent humans from annihilating it completely together with two or three adjacent star systems. Humans provide much of the necessary emission surplus for this to be possible, and they do so despite being fully aware of it ultimately leading to the complete extinction of their species. This circumstance is most fortunate, but it rests on a fragile balance of inherently human traits, behaviours and instincts most of us still know very little about. It is therefore of paramount importance that we do what we can to maintain this balance by carefully managing our interference levels.

Our scientists have a theory that if you heat up a planet slowly enough, its inhabitants will boil to death before they realise what is happening. So far humans have been most consistent in supporting this theory. Heating up Earth is an easy enough task, considering that this planet is actually already quite hot. Most of it is made of constantly boiling and unbearably smelly lava. Humans aren't very fond of lava and prefer keeping to the planet's cooler parts around the surface, where they frequently freeze and therefore burn anything they come across in order to generate some heat. Humans love burning things. They pride themselves with being the first terrestrial species to have discovered fire. As a matter of fact, most terrestrial creatures have discovered fire long before humans, but unlike humans, they were intelligent enough to immediately put it out and took great precautions in order to never ignite it again.

~

The Animal Kingdom Minus One

Although this guidebook focuses exclusively on humans, they are only one of the nearly nine million living species inhabiting Earth. The anatomic variety of terrestrial creatures spans from single-celled fungi, similar to the Neptunian sound wave eating amoebae, to five-metre Japanese spider crabs bearing very close resemblance to the twenty-seventh emperor of the Fornax Empire, Lollobicon the Wide-Tentacled, born and raised on one of the solid satellites of the gas giant Keloriton in the HIP 13044 system in a working-class family of seventy thousand Hiponic vampire squids. Given this variety of organisms, it is quite puzzling why humans would expect aliens from foreign galaxies to look like skinny grey humans with oversized heads. And yet, judging by our observations of human cinematography and the endless plethora of phoney alien encounter testimonials, that does indeed seem to be the general expectation.

Humans are different from other animals in that they don't consider themselves to be an animal. Moreover, they appear to despise the mere idea of being one. You will notice that whenever a human calls another human an animal, they always do so with a grimace of distaste, as if stating this obvious fact suddenly made them aware of just how disgusting the biological composition of terrestrial mammals is. Similarly, if a human claims to be an animal lover, they usually mean that they are a lover of all animals except humans (although not necessarily in the way that the wording suggests). In practice, this means having a compulsive urge to slide one's hands along the body surface of other animals at every given opportunity – regardless of the danger it may present. Most animals reluctantly tolerate this behaviour in order to avoid being shot. Many humans also appear to extract pleasure from feeding other animals. This behaviour is rather unique, as no other mammal has ever been encountered feeding humans out of sheer amusement.

It is not entirely clear what type of creature human actually believe themselves to be, but we do know that by their own classification the human species is one of the seven so-called great apes (although the substance of their greatness is a matter of great debate among other primates). The great apes are very similar to each other, with almost a ninety-nine percent DNA structure overlap. Humans are the least advanced of the seven, as they are still incapable of achieving a sufficient level of physical and emotional satisfaction without spending a lifetime toiling and transforming natural elements into an infinite range of synthetic appliances.

~

Distinguishing Humans from Other Apes

All apes tend to look alike to us extraterrestrials, which explains the surplus of mistakenly abducted baboons that have been roaming our Lunar labs for decades. It also explains the low success rates of our early infiltration attempts, where roughly every third infiltrator who tried to pass as a human eventually ended up in a human concentration camp for terrestrial fauna (commonly known among humans as a "zoo").

It wasn't until the famous pioneer infiltrator Zorn, who had involuntarily spent twenty-four years at a circus working undercover as a talking chimpanzee, had accidentally set himself on fire that we had learned about the importance of body hair length as a distinguishing feature between humans and other apes. (This distinction is less prominent in the Mediterranean region of the planet, which is why it is important to make a holistic assessment of various factors when trying to tell whether an ape is a human or not.)

One generic distinguishing feature of a human is wrapping. Unlike other species, humans have a habit of wrapping their bodies in various fabric materials for reasons which will be further explained in a subsequent chapter. This habit is so pronounced that it may take a lot of effort to ever find a human who is unwrapped. Although this may present some complications when performing intrusive research on abducted human subjects, it does make humans quite easy to identify. Wrapping on an ape means that it is most likely a human (infiltrator Zorn after his circus fire incident being one rare exception).

Another distinguishing human feature is an erect body stance. Any other ape spending more than one hour standing fully erect on two appendages in a booth holding a rifle would most likely be under some serious substance influence.

With that said, humans are fully capable of both standing and moving about on four appendages, which is something they often do when attempting to procreate. This is where it usually gets difficult, as humans often lack wrapping when doing so and produce sounds that are very hard to distinguish from those commonly made by other apes. If you happen to be near the Mediterranean when observing this behaviour, your best bet at distinguishing the observed apes as humans would be to wait for one of them to light a cigarette or for a third one to blast in through the door and make loud aggressive noises in a strongly accusative tone.

The easiest way of distinguishing humans from the other six apes is by the flat electronic gadget humans always carry in their palm and stare at whenever undistracted. Each human has at least one such gadget with which they have a very special bond. The gadget frequently emits various ringing sounds. Among humanologists these sounds are commonly referred to as the "Rings of Power" for having the power to immediately disrupt any activity a human is engaged in.

The device is precious to the human, who is constantly drawn to it by an invisible force. When wielded, the device endows the human with super-human abilities. It enables them to find answers to questions far beyond the limits of their intelligence, to turn on lights and activate machines, to have fuel and transportation brought to them, to spy on other humans, to generate depictions of their own face that look far less nauseating than the real one and to solve problems which humans didn't know they had before this device was invented. Wielding this gadget also makes the human invisible to others around them – in the same way an ostrich becomes invisible when sticking its head into the sand. Much like for the ostrich, the world blurs away for the human when the gadget is active. It grows grey, dull and unintriguing. While becoming invisible to their surroundings and, in effect, completely unconscious of their environment, the human becomes highly visible to others who are in possession of similar gadgets – wherever in the world they may be. That includes our infiltrators, of course. This is why parting a human from this device is not advised, as it makes the human considerably harder to abduct and much harder to control. It also makes them unbearably cranky and annoyingly restless.

~

Human Relations With Other Species

Despite their moderate scientific advances, humans are quite oblivious about their own ignorance. For instance, it is quite common for humans to believe that they are more intelligent than plants. They simply cannot conceive the extreme complexity and sophistication of scheming required only to survive when your every move takes a decade to carry out. It is due to this unfortunate circumstance that terrestrial plants, despite their intellectual superiority, are often held captive inside the human habitat under abhorrently cruel conditions. A common human myth about plants supposedly being drawn to light originates from numerous observations of indoor plants trying to escape through the window at their natural pace before being turned around by their human captors and having to start over again.

Keeping other living organisms captive is something humans do a lot – for a variety of reasons. One reason is that captive organisms are much easier to both pet and mass-slaughter for fuel than free ones. Another reason is the humans' desire to assert their superiority over other species. This appears to be the sole purpose of the previously mentioned institution humans call a "zoo", where large predators are kept in cages and are daily teased with delicious-looking human children placed safely outside the cage, just out of the predators' immediate reach.

Out of all terrestrial mammals (the word "terrestrial" in this book refers to everything that originates from the planet Earth, and not merely from its dry land), humans feel the most resentment towards other humans, which happens to be a sentiment they share with the rest of the animal kingdom, save for dogs.

Dogs are a domesticated breed of wolves who, through generations of human-supervised breeding, have developed a bizarre submission fetish. Some humans have that fetish too. For instance, those who enjoy being enslaved by vicious unsympathetic beasts inside their own habitat are called "cat people" based on their most frequent choice of master. Although the human-dog relationship is known to be the opposite, it took our researchers a while to establish which species actually dominates which. While dogs are often observed licking the feet of humans, they appear to be in full control of the human walking and feeding habits. While dogs are more frequently seen obeying human orders than vice versa, they are almost never seen serving food to humans or picking up human droppings during a joint walk. Humans, on the other hand, seem obsessed with collecting dog droppings. As soon as any are produced, humans tend to immediately pick them up, carefully place them in a plastic bag, tie the bag up for better protection and put it away in a special container – presumably for storage or ageing.

As for non-mammals, the human hostility towards other terrestrial species seems to positively correlate with the number of the target organism's appendages. The numerous reports on acts of unprovoked human violence against spiders has recently placed Earth at the top of the galactic list of planets recognised as unsafe for arthropods.

Microorganisms are another common object of unprovoked human hatred. One of the cruellest known human practices is to inject a small number of weakened viruses or bacteria into the human bloodstream only for them to be brutally slaughtered by overwhelming numbers of killer blood cells – merely as an exercise of their defence skills.

For the reasons mentioned, other Earth animals typically avoid humans. There are a few exceptions. Pigeons, for instance, are known to frequently manifest their protest against the human yoke in a manner most embarrassing by all codes of human conduct.

Being extremely unpopular among other animals, most humans are humbly aware of their inherent wickedness and often use being human as an excuse for having done something bad. They have even invented a term for it called a "human error" – a type of misconduct which could not have been possible had the creature that committed it not been a human. Few other terrestrial animals exhibit the same level of humility with regard to their own fallibility. You will never encounter a saltwater crocodile who will try to excuse its most recent proof of poor character by saying, "I am only a saltwater crocodile." But be prepared to hear the phrase "I am only human" a lot during your infiltration mission.

~

THE ORIGINS OF THE HUMAN PROBLEM

Roughly two hundred thousand years ago Earth was an agricultural colony of the Eternian Star Empire. The prime imperial species, hemans, genetically synthesised humans in their own image and started breeding them as what they hoped would be a natural cure against Neanderthal overpopulation. On the positive side – it did work. Although the pendulum may have swung a bit too far, some Neanderthal heritage still remains in the human species thanks to a number of prehistoric involuntary celibates who managed to skilfully exploit the inherent naivety and compassion of Neanderthals (historically known among humans as Homo Stupidus). It is this heritage that has enriched the human DNA with chromosomes for irregular bodily hair growth and an inherent fascination with graffiti. The replacement also helped confirm a hypothesis we developed at the end of our dinosaur eradication programme, suggesting that for every terrestrial species you suppress an even worse one will inevitably emerge.

With time, the heman species went extinct, its empire disintegrated and all knowledge about humans was gradually lost, together with two thirds of all sentient life in the galaxy and all of its main institutions, whose survival highly depended on all the self-destruction buttons of the heman-made galactic security network not being pressed simultaneously. As the galactic institutions were gradually re-established centuries later, it was decided that all knowledge on the human species (which had evidently inherited the dangerous heman predisposition to press unfamiliar buttons) had to be acquired anew.

So little was left that even humans themselves appeared to have lost the accurate storyline about their origins. Numerous competing and highly speculative human theories on how the genesis of their species came about emerged instead. The most popular ones suggest that the first human was not genetically designed, but rather crafted by hand from primitive materials in the image of an entity that doesn't have a body. The entity then supposedly ran out of primitive materials and had to mutilate the human in his sleep and use his body parts as building blocks to shape the second human, which turned out slightly smaller than the first due to material shortage. The two then had to procreate through incest until some offspring stopped showing up at anniversary parties and could thus no longer be considered family.

There are also theories about humans evolving from another ape species through evolution. That species did, in fact, exist. We named it Homo Erectus, following a particularly awkward encounter with infiltrator Zorn – one that is said to have inspired the latter to urgently get himself re-assigned to study the Hetero Impotentus species instead. (Unfortunately for Zorn, the latter did not last for more than a generation.)

So far, the only way the human species has been able to grow its aggregated knowledge is by artificially transferring it between generations. The success rate of this method has generally been less than modest – for a number of reasons. One is that every now and then, groups of humans tend to run amok and destroy everything around them, including all sorts of valuable heritage, for reasons no extraterrestrial intelligence has ever been able to comprehend. Another reason is that humans seem to be interested the least in things that matter the most. But mainly it is because humans are hopelessly bad at remembering to save their work and back up their memory drives.

Unlike hive-minded creatures, who complement the hive's compounded knowledge and make the hive infinitely wiser than its individual members, humans are infinitely dumber as a horde than they are as individuals. This, together with the eagerness with which they blew a couple of hundred thousand specimens of its own kind off the planet immediately after having learned to split atoms, is the reason why no intelligent extraterrestrial species has yet found it desirable to establish direct contact with this species.

This is also why the Human Infiltration Programme is the only one of its kind in the galaxy that admits agents with IQ levels below 500.

Zorn search party telepathic intercom transmission excerpt 1

Transmitted 20 seconds after the search party was teleported to Zorn's latest known location, injected into the two closest human bodies available, erasing the host human's mind and replacing it with their own consciousness.

Balbooza: *[Gee, do you copy?]*
Gee: *[Affirmative.]*
Balbooza: *[Is your gravity working?]*
Gee: *[No, it's off. Made an exception just for me. Everyone else is firmly attached to the planet's surface, while I am freely floating about and making gracious pirouettes.]*
Balbooza: *[What? Really?]*
Gee: *[Of course the bloody gravity is working! What kind of question is that?!]*
Balbooza: *[Sorry, it's just that I have never experienced gravity before…]*
Gee: *[I do not have a lever on my human suit that controls*

the spin rate of the planet, if that is what you are suggesting.]

Balbooza: [I think I've got some kind of lever on my human suit, but I'm not sure what it does.]

Gee: [Why don't you pull it then and we will know.]

Balbooza: [I am not sure how. It is underneath some intricate fabric my lower body is wrapped in.]

Gee: [Trousers, probably. Are there any humans around?]

Balbooza: [I think there are some, yes.]

Gee: [Then don't pull that lever just yet. What are the humans doing?]

Balbooza: [I am not sure. Most of them seem to be attached to surrounding vegetation.]

Gee: [What do you mean by "attached"? What exactly are they doing?]

Balbooza: [It is hard to tell. Some are sitting on the vegetation. Others are hanging. They also have their levers out. Some are pulling at them.]

Gee: [That doesn't sound quite right.]

Balbooza: [They are scratching themselves a lot. And each other. One is scrubbing the floor. That last one is the ugliest of them all and is wrapped in fabric.]

Gee: [Aren't they all wrapped in fabric?]

Balbooza: [No, just the ugly one scrubbing the floor. The rest aren't wearing anything.]

Gee: [Listen, Balbooza, I have no idea what kind of bizarre place that Zorn fellow ended up in before his comms went dead, but it sounds like you need to get out of there right now.]

Balbooza: [I am not sure I can. It looks like I am in a cage.]

Gee: [That's it, I'm calling the mothership and telling them to beam you back up immediately.]

Balbooza: [Wait. Maybe those humans are just hot. I mean, they've got an awful lot of fur.]

Gee: [Fur?]

Balbooza: [Yes, they are very hairy. Except for the ugly one scrubbing the floor. With this one I cannot tell for sure because of all the wrapping…]

Gee: [Wait. Are you saying that you are in a cage with very furry humans who are hanging from surrounding vegetation with their levers out and scratching each other?]

Balbooza: [Yes, that sounds about right. Except for the ugly one…]

Gee: [Are there any humans outside the cage?]

Balbooza: [Quite many, actually. All of them wrapped in fabric and pointing their limbs at me.]

Gee: [Balbooza, be honest with me: have you read your manual on humans before going on this mission?]

Balbooza: [Well, I have browsed through some of the main parts…]

Gee: [It's a two-pager! They haven't gotten around to making a proper manual because the department thought it would be cheaper to just keep sending Zorn down here, and he seemed to have gotten the hang of it already.]

Balbooza: [It's just that I'm not much of a reader. I prefer learning by doing, like the great Zorn.]

Gee: [Oh, I see. You are sent to an alien planet on a secret rescue mission to work undercover as a creature you don't know a single thing about in its natural environment. Could there possibly be a better opportunity to learn by doing?]

28

Balbooza: *[My thoughts exactly!]*

Gee: *[Brilliant. I am guessing that those "main parts" of the manual you have browsed through were not the parts that explain how to tell a human from a chimpanzee?]*

Balbooza: *[I don't believe they were, no.]*

Gee: *[Then let us do it your way and learn by doing. What is the most defining feature of a human – that first thing every infiltrator needs to know about humans before getting admitted to the programme?]*

Balbooza: *[Oh, that I know! They always stare at flat hand-held devices.]*

Gee: *[Exactly. And are those hairy humans in your cage staring at flat hand-held devices?]*

Balbooza: *[No. But the ugly one scrubbing the floor is. Impressive how he does that having so few limbs...]*

Gee: *[That is because the other ones are not humans, you lazy illiterate blob of radiation! You're in a cage with chimpanzees. Probably in a zoo. The ugly one must be a cage janitor. It's all in the manual. Humans put other animals in places like this to humiliate and tease them. This explains why I'm in a pool wearing some prehistoric amphibious equipment and this sulky walrus is staring right at me. We're both in a zoo.]*

Balbooza: *[Zoo... What a strange word... Any sign of Zorn?]*

Gee: *[Not unless a sulky walrus is a sign of Zorn. But I think I might have an idea about what Zorn was doing here...]*

Balbooza: *[Really? What's that?]*

Gee: *[Look down at the body you are wearing. Is it as hairy*

29

as the ones who are attached to the surrounding vegetation?]

Balbooza: [Might be a bit hairier even.]

Gee: [Just as I thought. Those bozos at the teleportation unit injected you into a chimpanzee. Wouldn't have surprised me with the kind of "talents" we've been attracting ever since HR pushed through that new inclusiveness policy, but somehow I don't think that this is a pure rendezvous of incompetence and coincidence...]

Balbooza: [I guess it's hard to be precise at beaming if you are light-sensitive...]

Gee: [You said your chimp is wearing trousers. That explains why those spectators were pointing their ugly limbs at you. Most humans wear trousers all the time, but I read that for some reason they find it extremely entertaining when other animals wear them, which they seldom do... Unless they are an alien infiltrator who believes to be wielding a human body.]

Balbooza: [I'm not sure I follow.]

Gee: [Look, before the programme had the budget for body injection beam teleporters, they would beam down infiltrators who were wearing artificial human suits. Zorn usually bought his in discount stores in order to save some allowance money. More than once he had accidentally bought costumes of other primates. I read his logs. He never really fully learned how to tell all these apes apart. He must have made the same mistake again when selecting the injection target this time. That explains the trousers. Humans wear clothes – Zorn knew this much.]

Balbooza: [So Zorn was wielding this chimpanzee body? Then how come I am wielding it now?]

Gee: [When your injection target was selected, it was supposed to be the closest vacant body to Zorn's last known location. So Zorn must have vacated it himself somehow. Probably he realised it was a monkey and had to quickly find himself a new host. The last time Zorn mistakenly went undercover as a chimpanzee he got stuck in a circus for twenty-four years, so he may have had to act quickly and used his remaining teleportation energy surge to jump bodies, leaving his transponder inside the chimp. That's why we could only trace him this far.]

Balbooza: [So how are we going to find him without the transponder?]

Gee: [Well, provided that Zorn wants to be found, he should be somewhere close by. He cannot just hover around in his natural form without giving himself away to humans, so he has to be wearing a host body. Without the transponder, it could be literally anyone around and we wouldn't know. So perhaps our best shot at finding Zorn is to help Zorn find us.]

Balbooza: [But we cannot hover around in our natural form either, and if we are wearing terrestrial host bodies, then without the transponder he will not be able to tell who we are.]

Gee: [That's why we'll have to work with anything terrestrial that he would recognize as potentially alien and assume it safe to make contact.]

Balbooza: [Do you have anything in mind?]

Gee: [As a matter of fact, I do.]

Balbooza: [What?]

Gee: [You.]

Balbooza: [Me?]

Gee: [Yes. Your chimpanzee outfit is Zorn's last known host. If he sees it in any context other than scratching its crotch inside this cage, he will realise something is going on. Now, let's get you out of that cage and somewhere a chimp wouldn't normally be.]

Balbooza: [But wouldn't humans get suspicious if they saw a chimpanzee walking about?]

Gee: [We'll have to dress you up a bit to make you look like a human. Shouldn't be that hard. These two species are almost identical, and you already have the trousers, so let's just find you a flat hand-held device and you'll look as human as they come.]

Balbooza: [Are you sure about this?]

Gee: [Do you have a better plan?]

Balbooza: [No...]

Gee: [Then let's get going. This grumpy walrus is getting uncomfortably close.]

Chapter 2

The Human Body and How to Wield It

W hen infiltrating a human society, you will have to assume a human body, which, sadly, happens to be one of the most impractical pieces of equipment in the universe. The human body only has four appendages with joints that only bend one way. The two lower appendages must be constantly used to keep the body from being squashed against the planet's filthy and germ-infested surface by the extreme Earth gravity. (This level of gravity was deliberately imposed by the galactic authorities several millennia ago after multiple neighbour complaints. Although it is quite effective in keeping humans away from other planets, terrestrial gravity does make our covert operations a lot more challenging.) These appendages are called "legs" and are equipped with two bizarrely shaped and dreadful-smelling pads called "feet" at the extremes. Feet are the only parts of the human body that regularly have contact with Earth, and which we believe to be the primary cause of Earth being so indecently dirty. The smell of human feet is closely related to the smell of a popular human food called "cheese", which is produced through the same fermentation process as the one taking place around human feet, only applied to the products of cow metabolism.

For an appendage that is expected to carry the specimen's full body weight, human feet are strangely soft and fragile. It is still unclear how humans managed to survive in the world before they invented shoes. You will, at times, be tempted to work undercover as a cow just out of sheer comfort, but please remember that posing as a cow on a planet infested by humans requires additional security measures. The aforementioned products of cow metabolism humans use to produce cheese are seldom voluntarily donated. The process of extracting them is extremely intrusive to the cow's integrity, but even that is only a mild inconvenience compared to what humans do to cows who are no longer useful for cheese production.

Human legs can only sustain the weight of the body for a limited period of time, at which point it would be natural for any quadrupedal animal to simply switch its weight over to its second pair of appendages. With humans, this seemingly simple and logical operation works less than perfectly. Frontal human appendages are optimised for groping, pointing and handing over stolen items, but they are excruciatingly unfit for moving about on the planet's surface. Even short walks can be very challenging for beginners, and we would definitely not recommend it for commuting or long distance marathons. Besides, as was once demonstrated by the legendary infiltrator Zorn's improvised attempt to downplay his leg malfunction when parading together with a Scottish bagpiper band, walking on hands attracts way too much human attention – especially when wearing a skirt.

The human body is so poorly designed that in order to avoid plunging against the planet's surface when the motoric power of all appendages has become exhausted, humans have had to build special appliances just to be able to uphold an erect enough posture for fuels to pass down their oesophagus. Such appliances are called "chairs" or "stools", and they can be effectively used as traps thanks to their tremendous ability to attract humans, who voluntarily settle their most vulnerable parts straight onto them. Infiltrator Zorn once famously set a whole new abduction quota standard by integrating his probing device directly into chairs, thereby relieving himself of the necessity to beam his abduction targets all the way up to the mothership and back.

Being aware of the limitations and flaws of the human body is essential for your success as an infiltrator. Although human appendages are not nearly as useful as regular suction-cupped tentacles, having so few of them can effectively prevent humans from passing through doors that have more than two handles.

Use this to your advantage whenever you find yourself in need of some privacy.

Although you will find your mobility to be severely arrested by the constraints of the human body, you must do your utmost to resist the temptation to bend those joints freely and move about using all four appendages. As was painfully learned by infiltrator Zorn during one of his weaker moments, failing to do so will immediately get you exposed and a male human in a black cloak with a cross in his hand chanting verses in a dead human tongue will be assigned to annoy you for the rest of your stay.

~

The Aesthetics of Human Hideousness

Humans frequently apply the concept of beauty to their bodies. You may find it counterintuitive at first that humans, being known as one of the most hideous and repulsive species in the galaxy, may be regarded as anything but infinitely ugly. However, working under-cover as a human you will need to accept that there can be multiple shades of grey, and even if no human has ever been rated as anything higher than one on a ten-point beauty scale by any sentient creature, you should keep an open mind and consider using decimals.

The human understanding of beauty when it comes to the human body appears to change over time and is very much defined by the average appearance of humans who are frequently visible to others. The fact that these humans usually have a very atypical appearance explains why the vast majority of humans think of themselves as inadequate. You can effectively use this circumstance to manipulate humans into liking you by pretending to find them beautiful. This, however, requires both skill and knowledge, so make sure to read the following section carefully.

Determining which bodily characteristics humans may find beautiful is hard and follows no obvious logic. One relatively common denominator is that humans are believed to be perceived as more beautiful the less they look like other animals. This explains why humans often shave off the fur on the parts of their body where other well-known animals have a lot of it. It also explains why humans pierce additional holes in their bodies and hook metallic objects into them. Very few other animals do that. (Some fish do, but not without human assistance.)

Despite apparently finding other animals very ugly, humans may sometimes pretend otherwise. For instance, infiltrators have often reported hearing humans call a horse or a dog beautiful. However, when the same humans are told that they look like that same horse or dog, they tend to act as if their initial assessment was inaccurate. Strangely, pointing out the opposite may insult them too. Infiltrator Zorn once ran a bar experiment, where he tried courting a sequence of human females by complimenting them on how little resemblance they bore to various domestic and wild fauna. This behaviour was reportedly met with less than little gratification. Zorn's conclusion was that the reaction may have been a result of the females sensing a lie, as many of them did in fact bear strong resemblance to the livestock he compared them to – a lie he immediately felt compelled to confess in an attempt to remedy the awkwardness of the situation. Still, it is advised that you avoid comparing humans to other animals unless you mean to insult them.

Humans are generally easily insulted by comments regarding their appearance. You can enrage these creatures simply by pointing out their most obviously defining bodily characteristics. For example, pointing out to a human with luxuriously furry elbows that her elbows are luxuriously furry is very likely to be taken as an insult, despite being unambiguously true. (If you have a practical reason for pointing it out – for example, if the elbow fur of a human sitting next to you on a bus[1] and reading a widespread newspaper[2] tickles your nostrils – consider addressing the problem without verbalising it. Try to discreetly trim or shave the fur off whenever an elderly human female boards the bus, which is when sitting humans are most likely to fixate their eyes on their papers and screens.)

Humans generally have less fur than other primates

---

[1]. A slow-moving metallic capsule used for enabling effective bacterial transmission between human hosts.

[2]. A summary of the most recent human misfortunes and misdeeds printed on flattened and badly bleached tree cadavers sized for maximum inconvenience.

and they tend to shave off most of whatever fur they have, except for one specific area on top of their heads, where the appearance and plenitude of hair is something they are absolutely obsessed about. It is important to locate this area accurately, as planting this much hair on any other area of your body will most certainly get you the wrong kind of attention.

Human males intentionally remove the hair from their faces by dragging sharp blades along their skin every day. Not doing so is called "wearing a beard". Be sure to wear it in the lower part of the face. Avoid wearing it altogether when operating a female body. Although it could sometimes provide effective protection against unsolicited male attention, it is also very likely to significantly weaken your stealth. Human males are generally terrified by any hair growing anywhere on female bodies except on the top of the head (almost as much as they are terrified of the absence of hair on the top of the female's head). Human females are a lot more courageous when it comes to hair, but tend to remove most of their own out of consideration for the males.

The distribution of hair on the rest of the human body surface is a very complicated matter that doesn't seem to follow any sensible pattern. Our century-long efforts to decode the evolutionary logic behind human body hair growth have been utterly unsuccessful. The only scientific paper published on the subject was infiltrator Zorn's study of internal human hair growth, which concluded that hair does not grow on the inside of the human body, even if deliberately planted and carefully nurtured. The paper received very poor reviews and the Human Hair Growth Evolution Research Programme at the Sirius University had all its funding withdrawn within a week after the paper was published.

A safe way of pointing out a human's defining bodily characteristic without eliciting the anger of its holder is by describing the characteristic as beautiful. Just be mindful that this may not work for all parts of the human body. Infiltrator Zorn has reported that complimenting humans on their beautiful pimples, humps and wrinkles has not been received well, as well as complementing body parts that weren't clearly visible at the time of the compliment. You should definitely avoid describing the pancreas or any other internal organs as beautiful, or at all, unless you are operating as an undercover surgeon. (In such cases, please bear in mind that any audible response to a compliment on a human's internal organ – be it gratitude or protest – may be a sign that the patient isn't properly sedated.)

The slimy white globes speckled with blood vessels and a pulsating dark spot sunk into the human head and partially covered with wrinkly patches of skin with a fringe of shallow spiky hairs are called "eyes" and are often claimed to be the most beautiful part of the human body. Our observations, however, suggest otherwise, as humans who constantly wear sunglasses appear to be more popular than those who don't. The purpose of eyes is to scan one's surroundings and transmit the collected data about everything that is going on as simplified two-dimensional visual images which the primitive human mind is able to comprehend.

Humans call what their eyes do "seeing", even though in reality their eyes only pick up a fraction of what is in front of them and pass it on to the brain as something entirely different. When seeing a thick layer of minced rock, strongly diluted with products of animal metabolism, decomposed corpses and infested with tentacle-like plant roots, insect eggs, fungi and bacteria in a densely packed layer beneath the human's feet, what human eyes transmit to the human's brain is "solid ground". When seeing rays of cancerogenic ultra-violet radiation breaking through Earth's gradually contracting ozone layer, the report from the eyes to the brain is usually "nice weather".

To the great advantage of our infiltrators, human eyes are only able to register information placed on surfaces immediately facing them. With the exception of some transparent materials, they are completely unable to see beyond any surface. Also, much like the eyes of the Tyrannosaurus Rex, one of the most easily distracted creatures that has ever roamed Earth, human eyes are constantly overstimulated by mobile devices and often fail to register slow and discrete objects that appear next to fast-moving colourful ones. This is why we always use juggling clowns to distract human parents while we abduct their children at birthday parties.

It is worth noting that few humans actually know what they look like, because the second humans are faced with a mirror or a picturing device they immediately try to look like someone else. It took many years before we understood that the imagery intel we have been gathering from human communication networks for decades was strongly biased. Apparently, humans don't actually spend most of their time frozen in a twisted posture, holding two fingers up in the air and stretching their faces.

Unfortunately, this ignorance about their own appearance doesn't make our undercover work any easier, as humans are extremely attentive to what *other* humans look like. They don't need to suspect you of being an alien to constantly scrutinise your appearance in search of weak spots. Our research shows that finding weaknesses in other humans' appearance makes humans feel better about themselves.

Thus, if you want to avoid too much human attention, make sure to choose an ugly host body. Don't be fooled by the common human belief that ugly humans are beautiful on the inside. After having inspected thousands of abducted human bodies our scientists have arrived at the unanimous conclusion that all humans are at least as ugly on the inside as they are on the outside.

Human bodies are covered with a waterproof elastic tissue called "skin". It has the remarkable ability to regenerate itself if pierced and its colour appears to be strongly correlated with manners of communication, choice of apparel and life expectancy. Some humans have opinions about humans with a certain skin colour being better than others. You may rest assured that such beliefs are completely misguided. Our own research has confirmed time and again that all humans are equally awful.

~

The Zero Sum Gas Exchange

The purpose of human nostrils has been the subject of centuries of research and a great deal of heated debate, occasionally spawning intergalactic wars that led to the destruction of more than a dozen star systems and utter annihilation of several trillion species, before a fragile consensus could be established that human nostrils are likely there for breathing. The most hardlined sceptics frequently pointed to the absence of an evolutionary logic that could justify having two minor holes that should have the exact same purpose as a larger one next to them. It was only after having studied human mating behaviour in more detail that the nowadays prevalent theory was developed. It suggests that any opening in the human body that can be expanded wider than an inch appears to be at risk of finding itself penetrated with a variety of objects for purposes too alien for us to comprehend. If applied to breathing openings, such penetration would create a suffocation hazard. The fact that evolution has indulged humans with two small nostrils rather than with one large one perfectly supports this theory.

Breathing is a rather useless exercise, during which a mixture of atmospheric gases, exhaust fumes, bacteria, tiny insects, organic decomposition particles and occasional sperm cells from plants, enters the human body – and then leaves it again, enriched with an aerosol sample of the content of the given human's digestive system. The gas mixture always enters in a consistent manner through the nose or mouth, but the release happens through a variety of methods, which appear to be structured in a social hierarchy, evoking very different responses from surrounding humans.

Releasing the gas the same way it came in is called "breathing out" and will normally not evoke any response at all, unless the release is directed right into the face of another person – especially after a period of intense alcoholic intoxication.

Other air release methods appear to evoke condemnation and resentment among surrounding humans – even when the release isn't immediately directed into the breathing holes of others. However, if such releases are accompanied by loud sounds, they suddenly appear to evoke great joy and laughter. Make sure to use this to your advantage when trying to win human affection.

On the whole, we haven't been able to identify any practical use from letting gases pass in and out of the human body, which is why human breathing is considered to be a zero sum gas exchange, most likely devised to catch the mixed-in particles with human mucous membranes in order to prevent excessively long life.

The Mystery of Humanium

One of the greatest challenges our scientists have faced throughout the millennia of human studies has been the effort to determine the main purpose of the human organism's operation. At the core of the human body there is a rather sophisticated metabolic mechanism built to convert fuel into organic products of a most suspicious kind. With humans, more or less any organic matter appears to work as fuel, but the output is always the same. Because this element appears to be the only universally generalisable product of human existence, it was given the name "humanium".

The purpose of humanium is still unclear, but it is believed to be immensely significant to humans. The whole architecture of urban human infrastructure appears to revolve around the collection, transportation and storage of humanium. Every modern human habitat is connected to a pipeline system that effectively collects humanium from residents and transports it to an unknown destination. No infiltrator has so far volunteered to follow the trail of humanium far enough to know exactly where it leads, but infiltrator Zorn's theory is that all humanium eventually reaches a designated storage area, where it rests and compounds for many years, supposedly waiting for its day to be put to use – whatever that may be – and thereby reveal to the rest of the galaxy the true purpose of human existence.

For a while it was believed that humanium is an energy source, especially when test results from storage facilities revealed abnormally high methane levels. Infiltrator Zorn was dispatched to collect more samples for our field laboratories to examine, but the mission had to be aborted after Zorn was detained by human police when trying to smuggle ten kilograms of humanium onto a human aircraft. The famous infiltrator felt the cargo was too precious to travel as checked in luggage, but reported that he wasn't duly informed by the personnel of the low-cost airline he was travelling with that the hand luggage limit was only eight kilograms. The mission was nearly compromised when Zorn was apprehended while attempting to distribute the excessive two kilograms of humanium into various pockets of his human outfit.

Today, the scientific opinions are divided on the subject of humanium. Half of the galactic scientific community believes its purpose to be strictly religious, while the other half is inclined to view it as part of some ingenious self-destruction. The fact that all the methane dense and therefore highly inflammable humanium transportation networks are situated underneath human settlements supports this theory. Although most of the galactic community sincerely hopes for the latter to be true, a lot more research is needed, and a lot more humanium needs to be smuggled.

The Horrors of Human Reproduction

Like most Terrestrial organisms, humans only have two sexes. However, much like in human grammar, there are many exceptions to the rule and even the primary two sexes may, at times, not be easy to tell apart.

For some reason, humans often get offended when directly asked to specify their sex, which leaves us aliens with very few certain clues. A common rookie mistake is to use human restroom signs as guidance on what distinguishes a male body from a female one. Doing so may leave you with a false expectation that a human female is supposed to look like a rocket shaped cone on legs. Our interpreters have been able to derive that the cone actually represents the fact that human females often wear garments that are a lot looser and easier to remove than those usually worn by males. Despite plentiful empirical evidence supporting this, our infiltrators have reported numerous incidents where assessing the sex of the human by this characteristic has resulted in unpleasant surprises.

A more certain method of determining a human's sex is by examining their profile on imaginary life simulators humans call "social media", where the sex of a human can often (but not always) be derived from the

47

pronouns listed in the human's profile description. Even if no pronouns are listed there, you may still get some clues from the human's profile picture. Examine the photo for the presence of such clues as a tilted head, flowers, a large fish or the person in the photo being a cat. They are usually very gender-specific, and a human's gender often correlates with the human's sex. (The concept of gender has been added to all post-millennial editions of this handbook and will be further explained in a later chapter.)

A very common extraterrestrial infiltrator mistake is to assume that the person behind a social network user profile photo featuring a cat is, in fact, a cat. Nothing can be further from the truth. Such a profile image merely indicates which cat the human slave using it belongs to.

The most certain way of telling the sex of a human is by examining the human's genitals. Genitals are a set of reproductive organs of varying sizes and shapes that appear to largely control the rest of the human body. Getting to examine them may, at times, pose certain challenges. Humans are extremely secretive about those parts of their body and avoid exposing them to other humans by all means available. They even have a special name for those who don't.

Our focus group research has often shown that many humans find the mere sight of other humans' genitals deeply disturbing. So much, in fact, that most human parents believe that their children can be trau-matised by seeing an adult human's reproductive organs. However irrational you may think this is, please do not try to prove them wrong.

Our scientists are still debating the root causes of this suspicious human fear of that one specific part of the human body. The most popular theory suggests that it stems from a primaeval instinct that drives human defence systems to identify furry and ambiguously shaped figures as potential forest predators. This fear is believed to be the reason why humans are generally tremendously ashamed of their bodies. They cover their bodies in garments when appearing in public and panic when accidentally exposed.

Strangely, humans tend to feel a lot less uncomfortable being seen undressed by other animals than by humans. Beware that this may not apply to all animals, as was proven by infiltrator Zorn, who once attempted entering a human female dressing room disguised as a bear. His new infiltration gear test report was very disappointing.

Your best chance of making good use of the above method for determining a human's sex is by visiting a public restroom. Do not get confused by the name – human restrooms are very ill-equipped for rest. Even our best infiltrators have seldom managed to get more than twenty minutes of quality sleep in a public restroom before an unfamiliar human would seize the opportunity to determine their sex or confuse them with a humanium depository. Our observations suggest that the primary purpose of visiting public restrooms lies in expressing one's creativity through various forms of wall art, unauthorised passive and active smoke and fume inhalation, face painting, as well as admiring one's own reflection in very large mirrors. All of these services are paid for in body liquids, usually in advance and without a return policy.

In the absence of a public restroom, determining the sex of humans becomes ever more challenging. Investigation by groping typically only works in confined spaces with only a few humans of inferior physical build and social status present. Only infiltrators working undercover as world leaders and film producers have so far been able to effectively pull this off. Infiltrator Zorn's report on quick sex assessment by grabbing around in the crowd convincingly proved the inadequacy of this method for infiltrators who plan to keep using their human host body after the assessment is over.

When you've run out of options, your absolutely final resort in determining the sex of a human will have to be coupling. This requires some thorough explanation.

Unlike most intelligent species, humans are unable to pass on aggregated knowledge to their offspring due to the limitations of their procreation mechanism. Contrary to the more intelligent species of the Milky Way galaxy, coupling humans do not merge and divide into new specimens that inherit the combined knowledge of their parents. Instead, humans eject samples of their chromosomes containing only physiological data, which then merge together to spawn new humans that share random physical traits of their parents, but are blatantly stupid.

This presents a cyclically recurring challenge to a society aspiring to develop but consisting of individuals who mostly only live long enough to realise the purpose of pension funds. Humans address this through a process called "education". Education is supposed to enable knowledge transfer between generations, but is essentially a method of storing data in the human brain, with the share of data loss over time amounting up to 95 percent. The amount of data stored in the brain by the end of the average human's education roughly equals the amount of disk space required to install a human computer operating system from the early 21st century.

Unlike the operating system installation process, which takes roughly an hour, education usually takes between 15 and 25 years. This corresponds to 20-35 percent of an average human lifespan. The first eighteen years put an immense strain on the physical and mental health of the parents, whose continued temporary existence after offspring ejection is necessary to ensure the survival of their utterly incapable progeny.

Our research indicates that no creature inflicts more suffering upon humans than human children. As the average return on investment from having children is far below the average amount of suffering endured, it is puzzling why this species still continues to exist.

Some researchers attribute this paradox to the aforementioned memory data loss rate. Others point to the generally observed human obsession with youth. Our post-abduction experiments have shown that the affection humans display for other animals, human or not, varies proportionally to the target animal's age. While seemingly indifferent to very old specimens, humans peak in affection expressed when presented with very young ones, to a point where the human's facial muscles begin to contract in the most unnatural ways, the voice pitch peaks in frequency, speech defects begin to appear and communication turns nonsensical.

Although this behaviour is quite disturbing to observe, it appears that this state could be addictive to humans and thus spur further procreation as means of acquiring new objects of affection, as the prior ones grow older and thereby gradually lose their ability to produce the same levels of satisfaction.

In order to initiate the formation of a new human, chromosomes need to be passed from a male's body into a female one. The process works best when both bodies are human, sufficiently mature and alive. It only requires two humans and does not work when both are of the same sex.

You will notice that none of the above is obvious to all humans. Our scientists have had no trouble acquiring large volumes of video footage, widely available on human electronic data networks, which has provided plentiful insights into the mechanics of human mating. Apparently, humans extract great pleasure from watching other humans try to procreate.

Oddly, they seem to enjoy it more the more unsuccessful the procreation attempts appear.

After studying three million hours of such video material, our scientists have managed to finally establish that the most effective method of conception is for the male body to shoot out 23 chromosomes in a small autonomous drone programmed to carry them into the female body and dock. In order to be able to administer this transfer, a sudden increase in organic nationalism is required. Organic nationalism is when the cells in one human body part believe that they are entitled to more blood than others, causing an imbalance in blood supply that elevates an organ and makes it hard and resilient to atmospheric changes – a state evidently most fitting for dispatching chromosomes into other human bodies.

A cautious planner might say that having one or two spare chromosomes onboard a carrier drone might be a good habit in case the ride gets bumpy. Being an extremely risk-averse species, humans usually shoot out close to 200 million drones, each carrying 23 chromosomes, just to be sure that at least one will make it to the rendezvous point. Do humans really need to make such an immense investment in building up the odds this high? After having observed how ineffectively human chromosome drones are routed in all the publicly available human mating footage, our scientists unanimously confirmed that they do.

The human procreation process is extremely tiring, frustrating and painful, which is evident in the heartrending shrieks and moans humans emit when engaged in it. In order not to discourage further procreation (thereby threatening the long-term survival of the species) humans try to keep coupling practices hidden from their existing children.

In the rare cases when conception is completed successfully, which usually follows tens of billions of chromosome carrying drones being destroyed, a new human begins to form inside the female's body until it breaks out in a most horrific bloody scene. If you don't have any educational footage of this available, get a copy of the famous human film called *Alien*, known for one of the most xenophobic and stereotyping portrayals of extraterrestrials in human cinematography. The birth concept enacted there, featuring a tiny xenomorph breaking out of a human body, is very close to how human birth works, except for the output being a lot less noisy than regular new-born humans.

Most humans seem to have come to terms with the prospect of extreme suffering and health hazards required to produce more humans. Many human females even survive the ejection process with manageable levels of body elasticity maintained. Yet, merely observing this experience can be extremely traumatising. Many veteran infiltrators report still being haunted by nightmares of having little humans trying to break out of their bellies and then needing to be rolled around in wheeled padded wagons.

The effectiveness of human reproduction appears to be inversely correlated with wealth. The poorest humans are the most effective reproducers, while prosperous humans are typically a lot more effective at breeding other animals than they are at breeding humans. Before we had enough research, we assumed that the superiority of poor humans in producing children was a consequence of their inability to acquire food by any other means. However, deeper studies of happiness levels in different human social strata have led us to believe that humans enjoy being poor a lot more than being rich and therefore have a stronger desire to pass on their living experience to new generations.

The Junkyard of the Human Mind

The human brain is the second most powerful organ after genitalia in controlling the rest of the human body and its behaviour. Like most other terrestrial creatures, humans only have one brain. This limitation forces them to use it as a multipurpose device for controlling motoric bodily functions, information processing, data storage and reality distortion, none of which is handled particularly well.

The human brain's processing bandwidth is so low that it can only process one thought at a time. This makes humans convenient targets for covert operations. If you manage to grab and hold the attention of a human with something they find infinitely fascinating, like an aircraft crashing into a highrise or another human appearing without any fabric wrapping around their body, they will stay oblivious to virtually any change in their environment.

This shortcoming has long been effectively used by human pickpockets – a line of trade most convenient for professional alien infiltrators who prefer to perform intrusive research on human subjects on the go, without having to beam them up to the mothership first, second only to proctologists and cocaine smuggler instructors.

While the processing power of a human brain is vastly inferior even to the most primitive pocket calculator, its storage capacity is rather comprehensive and could have been quite useful – had it not lacked any kind of order or structure. Virtually all things a human sees, hears and thinks are recorded and stored in their brain as memories in a manner that makes them almost impossible to retrieve. Rather than being carefully sorted into chronologically or typologically organised folders, they appear to be randomly dumped into the vastness of inner human chaos.

The only semi-working method by which any desired memory can be deliberately retrieved from storage is to pull at a string of associated memories or objects, which themselves may need a great deal of luck if they are to be retrieved from the abyss of the human brain. Human memory retrieval is such an incredibly complicated business that many humans revert to measures as desperate as storing actual physical objects they associate with certain memories boxed in the attic of their habitat, because apparently these are much easier for them to find than the actual memories in their own heads.

The good thing about having a brain that stores everything a human sees and thinks is that you can retrieve any information you need from a human subject by means of a regular mind scan without having to suffer the pain of interacting with the subject. As you will quickly learn, receiving any information stored in a human brain by means of the human verbalising it into sonic signals is not only immensely tedious due to the extreme poverty of human vocabulary; it also poses a significant risk of data loss and distortion – often reaching a level of inaccuracy where not having received the information at all would have put you in a more knowledgeable position.

The downside of storing everything in the brain is that in order to retrieve any useful information you will have to scan through immense amounts of utterly useless nonsense and will occasionally bump into information regarding the human's personal hygiene and yet unexplored coupling behaviours you will strongly wish you hadn't come across. Infiltrator Zorn had to spend several centuries in intensive therapy after having made the rather rash decision to save himself some time by scanning the brains of a dozen Dominican monks instead of reading through their carefully hand-written parchment scrolls during his early Medieval infiltration mission. (Monks are humans who voluntarily abstain from procreation in order to make more room for begging a never-seen entity to give them strength in their abstinence.)

Zorn's mind scanning experiment made it clear why such divine strength was necessary for preventing whatever was appearing inside those monks' heads during various religious rituals from happening to real humans. Zorn no longer suffers panic attacks at the sight of robes, but the epileptic seizures triggered by the word "vespers" still prevent him from using classic Italian scooters as means of terrestrial transportation.

It is this toxic influence of certain human thoughts over the fragile minds of more intelligent species that has forced us to abandon the practice of mind scanning as a source of human intelligence and revert to classic interrogation methods, such as online personality tests and fake film auditions.

~

Diseases As Means of Transportation

When living among humans, you will sometimes hear of them contracting a certain disease. Contracts like this regard transportation services and are usually signed with groups of microorganisms (predominantly viruses and bacteria). The group in question is then allowed to use the human as a transportation vessel to reach other humans.

This is a convenient way of getting around and is much cheaper than renting or hijacking a whole human like we usually do. The downside, of course, is that you do not really control the human and may have to suffer from exposure to the occasional toxic substances humans like to inject into their bodies. Also, the lingo in this industry is rather confusing. The boarding process is called "infection". Disembarkation is referred to as "transmission". The remuneration to the transporting human is called "sick pay", because apparently humans transporting a virus are referred to as "being sick".

It is important to know that although it is much favoured by low-budget microorganism travellers, disease is not a family friendly travel method. The logistics inside the human body are typically less than perfect. Food and drinks are neither included, nor sold on board. This tends to catch frequent travellers, who are used to a certain level of comfort, completely off-guard. As the travel time from one human to another may last for at least half the average bacterium's lifetime, unaware travellers who haven't brought their own often find themselves in dire straits during the voyage and begin feeding on anything edible within their reach. Such feeding frenzies may cause substantial property damage to the human body. In extreme cases the body may break down entirely, creating significant travel delays for the remaining passengers.

Travellers who are caught feeding on their vessel are therefore dealt with by humans in the most decisive way. Specially trained killer cells are dispatched to eliminate such bacteria and viruses, and sometimes poison agents are injected into the human body to kill off the hungry. Both methods create a lot of collateral damage, with all viruses and bacteria bearing physical resemblance to the hungry berserkers being at risk of annihilation once the raid has begun. Due to this racial profiling, the human immune system has often been accused of systemic racism. Critics have also pointed to the fact that all the blood cells employed in the immune system are almost exclusively white.

Inconsistent as they are, humans also use the term "disease" for certain things that have absolutely nothing to do with transportation. Cancer, for instance, is a form of agriculture where microbial farmers generate crops by altering the composition of cells in human body tissue to produce artificial growth, much like what human farmers do with the composition of the habitable layers of Earth. While having a generally benevolent attitude towards the farmers gradually destroying their planet, fellow humans put millions of cancer farmers out of work every year by killing their crops with chemical weapons.

∾

THE HUMAN BODY AS IT SHOULD HAVE BEEN

Ultimately, the human body is the greatest constraint to human development – greater even than their primitive intellect and their morbid fascination with death and destruction. The main reason for this is that human evolution is no longer able to keep up with the artificially propelled changes in human lifestyle and society structure. Thanks to the now rather widespread and utterly absurd notion of human life having some kind of universal value, natural selection in human societies has stopped altogether.

Contemporary humans have made a cult out of preventing other humans from dying. Never before have bad genes had such an easy ride between human generations. Almost no disease or body defect is severe enough to kill a human before procreation has been made possible. Natural starvation still prevails in some areas of the planet, but even in these areas fewer humans starve to death than are being produced by the same parents with the same genes.

In effect, human bodies don't really change. Their colour palette variety gradually increases as human races mix, but the basic structure of the body remains the same. Combined with the rapid change constantly occurring in human societies, the human body grows increasingly incompatible with the human's natural environment.

Had it not been for the widespread human obsession with preventing other humans from dying, the human body would have evolved a lot faster and its design would by now be much more aligned with the contemporary human lifestyle. Standard inter-human communication would no longer be severely arrested thanks to much longer and significantly more agile thumbs able to reach every pixel of even the largest touchscreen within a matter of milliseconds. Slowthumbed humans would have gradually been eliminated through natural selection, as they would no longer have been able to keep up with conversations and compete for the chat bot's attention when trying to order food or call the ambulance.

Human minds would have developed the capability to process simultaneous information cues. The genes of those least capable of doing so would have gradually perished from existence as a result of overexposure to seizures, heart attacks and stress related impotence. Give it another millennium or two and humans might even have developed the capability of atomically splitting themselves, which would allow them to be in multiple places at once. They would then easily meet the societal expectations of succeeding in one's work while never failing to deposit and extract one's offspring from daytime confinement in a brainwashing facility, produce custom made fuel for one's co-habitants and inflict sufficient satisfaction upon one's spouse by effectively imitating intercourse.

All the above would, of course, have required substantially larger brains contained in substantially larger heads, the weight of which would have had to be supported by means of artificial appliances. This would have made all humans equal in sharing the same disability. With disabilities becoming increasingly fashionable among humans, such equality would surely have deescalated the currently growing tensions between those naturally gifted with disabilities and those who barely qualify as allergic, with nothing but a mild lactose intolerance to show for themselves.

A million years from now, if evolution would have kept up, humans would not only have been able to be in different places simultaneously, but also to be different people at different moments. They would have been able to be sensitive and fragile when their mate is in need of a compassionate audience, and then be strong and wilful when their mate is in need of protection or inspiration for creating new humans. They would have been able to be serious and focused when handling an important diplomatic negotiation, and then suddenly possess a sense of humour when speaking to humans who share that trait.

Had humans been allowed to continue evolving naturally, they would by now have developed the ability to tactically switch gender and sexual orientation in order to advance their careers by effectively evading various diversity policy filters. Humans with inflexible binary sexuality would have gradually been cancelled out of all means of life support and expelled from existence. A naturally gender-fluid and sexually diverse humanity would have been a lot easier for us to infiltrate. Instead, with the way things have developed, all infiltrators need to pass a multitude of tedious exams in human sexual codes and gender roles, which severely inflates the demand for handbooks such as this one.

You may feel a temptation to genetically modify your human host body in order to acquire at least some of the aforementioned characteristics before you infiltrate. However, as some of Zorn's mission reports have shown, doing so is likely to decrease your physical resemblance to a contemporary human to a level which, although seeming perfectly adequate to an alien, isn't nearly convincing enough to humans.

As a matter of fact, all known alien encounters humans have on record were encounters with alien infiltrators who were under the false impression of being indistinguishable from humans. There is simply no way of fitting an amount of brain substance that would fully satisfy your intellectual capacity into a human head without making it look entirely alien. Neither is it possible to accommodate a sufficient level of four-dimensional night vision without altering the design of human eyes to a degree that would set even the bravest human trembling in terror at the mere sight of you. Not to mention that grey – however well it goes together with just about any kind of apparel – is still a long way from becoming the standard skin colour it will be after all human races have ultimately been mixed out.

These unfortunate encounters have fuelled human imagination to produce the well-known and utterly bizarre stereotypes of extraterrestrial visitors who, despite having presumably originated from an entirely different star system, are expected to be a lot more similar to humans than humans are to 99% of all living organisms on Earth. Therefore, if you should succeed in seamless infiltration, you will have to make due with the extremely outdated, clumsy, intellectually arrested and evolutionarily indefensible contemporary human body design.

The upside of it is that having such an abhorrent pile of organic junk for a body should make it a lot easier for you to naturally behave in the imbecilic manner that commonly defines humans.

∽

Zorn search party telepathic intercom transmission excerpt 2

Transmitted 17 minutes after dispatch.

Balbooza: [*Could you tell me once again what I need to do?*]
Gee: [*Get up, slowly walk to the back door of the monkey cage and wait there until the janitor unlocks it. Then hit the janitor on the head with that tree branch and quickly run through the door. I'll be waiting for you on the other side.*]
Balbooza: [*Gee, this is a lot of information. Could you please take it slowly, piece by piece?*]
Gee: [*Get up.*]
Balbooza: [*How?*]
Gee: [*Elevate your chimpanzee body by unfolding your back appendages.*]
Balbooza: [*Which ones are the back appendages?*]
Gee: [*The short ones.*]

Balbooza: [*And how do I unfold them?*]

Gee: [*Er... I'm not sure how to explain this.*]

Balbooza: [*Never mind, I think it's working. There, now they are straight like laser beams!*]

Gee: [*Great. Are you standing up?*]

Balbooza: [*What's standing up?*]

Gee: [*The opposite of lying down.*]

Balbooza: [*What's—*]

Gee: [*Look, just try to assume the same posture as that ugly janitor, perpendicular to the planet surface.*]

Balbooza: [*Ok... I think I can do that. There.*]

Gee: [*What's that sound?*]

Balbooza: [*I don't know. All the humans around the cage are making it. They are pointing their appendages at me and the janitor, stretching their faces and making these awful sounds.*]

Gee: [*Maybe they suspect something. You need to hurry up. Walk over to the back door.*]

Balbooza: [*How do I walk?*]

Gee: [*Put one of your back appendages in front of the other, then lean on it, raise the second one up in the air... Oh, Space, this is too much!!! Just check if you can see any moving primates and mimic their movement!*]

Balbooza: [*Should I keep making this scrubbing motion with my front appendages while I walk?*]

Gee: [*What scrubbing motion?*]

Balbooza: [*You know, mimicking the janitor's posture, like you said I should do.*]

Gee: [*For the love of the galaxy, don't tell me you are standing next to the janitor wearing your chimp body*

66

and mimicking his every movement in front of a human crowd!]

Balbooza: [Not anymore. I'm mimicking the moves he was making before he stopped scrubbing and began staring disapprovingly at me.]

Gee: [Gracious stardust... Ok, you're clearly good at mimicking. Stop mimicking the janitor and start mimicking any chimpanzee you see moving about, only try to change your movement trajectory towards the back door.]

Balbooza: [Sure. I would need to remove those trousers first though. What they are doing cannot be done with trousers on.]

Chapter 3

Human Instincts and How to Fake Them

Ever since humans started circumventing the course of evolution, their behavioural patterns, instincts and values have grown increasingly incompatible with their current way of life. They have come quite far in understanding this fact, but not yet far enough to do anything substantial about it. Human genetic engineering hasn't yet advanced far enough for humans to be able to edit away unnecessary elements from the human genome.

One such element is the untimely production of adrenaline when none is needed. Adrenaline is a hormone a human produces when in a state of fear. Fear is a survival mechanism that prevents humans from engaging in hazardous behaviours which more intelligent species would have normally refrained from out of common sense. Adrenaline also helps humans run faster when faced with an immediate threat, such as when being approached by a lion, a charity fundraiser or by a male gorilla that has had its whole troop wiped out by human poachers three years earlier and hasn't mated since. In addition, adrenaline elevates the human's pain threshold in case the gorilla catches up.

Apart from that, adrenaline is all bad news. It makes humans loud, cranky, unfocused, even more irrational than usual, prone to panic and being intolerably annoying. Humans call the effect of intense adrenaline production "being scared" or "stressed", or "anxious". The difference between the three is not always apparent and it will take you a lot of practice before you can convincingly imitate these different variations of behaving stupidly. Here are some instructions that may help you along the way.

≈

How to Act Scared

Acting scared involves a set of facial gestures, sounds and body movements. The movements are the easy part, as they appear to be relatively random.

When scared, humans typically shrug their shoulders, fold their arms towards their face and shrink back with their upper body, sometimes amplifying the movement with a small backwards jump.

After that it is usually all improvisation.

You may feel free to move your limbs in any direction or trajectory, as long as you do it immediately after the expected source of fear has made itself apparent. If you wait for more than two seconds after the trigger event and then start waving your appendages the effect will not be the same. You shouldn't do it too early either, as that could reveal your superior predictive abilities to humans who, as you already know, are only able to properly predict events that have already occurred.

The jump is a good move, but try not to overdo it by jumping higher than the average human's physical capability dictates. Also, try not to jump towards the supposed threat, even if you realise that it isn't a threat to begin with.

Sounds are more specific. Humans have a set of shrieks saved exclusively for situations where they get suddenly spooked. These sounds are supposedly purposed for scaring off threats, although most of the threats we have surveyed find them annoying at most.

The shrieks you should use need to correlate with the sex of your human costume. Confusing male and female shrieks will bring about more questions than you will be willing to answer. The female shriek is a high frequency sound, similar to what humans would otherwise describe as similar to a "whistle". How any large predator should find it intimidating is hard to imagine, but it may slightly distort the predator's hearing during the meal, thus making it an easier prey for even larger predators.

Beware that "similar to a whistle" really is not the same thing as a whistle, so don't try to cheat your way through a violent assault by whistling. Infiltrator Zorn's reports indicate that such substitution is particularly counter-productive in situations where the assault is perpetrated by a pack of stray dogs.

The male scream is slightly harder to emulate, as it doesn't really sound like anything you may have heard elsewhere. The good news is that these screams vary so much that you may just be able to get away with improvisation. However tempting, do not try to cheat by using a female shriek when working undercover as a human male. It may damage your social network severely enough to endanger the success of your whole operation.

The facial gestures are the most important component of exhibiting fear. However well you wave your limbs, jump around and scream, if your facial expression is a display of joyful harmony, your pretence of fear will be as transparent as Earth's atmosphere was before humans discovered coal. On the other hand, if you master the skill of making a genuinely terrified face, you may still get away with standing perfectly still and silent.

The most important part is the eyes. Roll back the lids and try to squeeze your eyes out of your head without touching them. Don't let the eyeballs pop out of your head completely, as that would complicate matters in an array of ways, but just let it become apparent that your eyes are spherical. Pull the corners of your mouth backwards just a little bit while slightly opening the mouth. If your mouth looks like there is a small banana stuck in it sideways, then you are doing it right.

~

When to Be Scared

Now that you have learned the human art of looking scared, it is time to put your new skill into practise. This part will require a lot of learning by heart, because as we have established earlier, the variety of conditions under which human bodies start pumping out adrenaline is almost limitless. Older literature usually doesn't elaborate on these variations enough, simply stating that adrenaline is produced when the human is threatened. Since that is very rarely the case, let us instead focus on some of the most common scenarios. Here are some entirely non-threatening situations in which you should immediately start exercising your newly acquired skill of looking scared:

Seeing A Spider

Spiders are small furry beings with eight appendages and four pairs of eyes. Unlike most terrestrial creatures, spiders look unimpressively normal by galactic standards. These rather attractive creatures were the initial founders of what on Earth is known as the World Wide Web – a global network constantly disrupted by human-wielded brooms. The term has later been hijacked by humans, who now use it to label the human-made self-propelled (but not yet self-aware) instrument of mass psychosis.

Spiders are primarily known for two things: spinning webs and scaring the cosmic abyss out of humans. This effect they have on humans is almost as universally consistent as it is unintentional. Humans are terrified of simply seeing spiders, even at times when spiders are making little or no effort to appear scary.

It is a common myth that this effect is stronger on female humans. Male humans are at least as scared of spiders as the females, but this fear is largely overshadowed by the human male's much stronger fear of displaying cowardice in front of females, which is why males only scream and run at the sight of spiders when no female is present. If one is, they mobilise all the energy they can spare from their panicking body and channel it into a lethal strike against their petrifying adversary by means of a hand-held shoe. A courageous murder of an unarmed creature approximately one thousandth their own size often brings the male human great prestige in the eyes of any observing females. This effect is contingent on precision and wears off with every new strike and every new footstep shaped dirt mark on the walls of the female's habitat. Once relieved from the presence of the female, the victorious human males commonly spend hours curled up on the bathroom floor with their arms tightly embracing their heads, recovering their nervous systems from the shock of the spider encounter by sobbing uncontrollably and calling for their female parent.

Hearing a Startling Noise

Humans are very pessimistic about sudden noises. Although most such noises originate from entirely harmless things for entirely harmless reasons, humans always react to them as if they were omens of approaching death, and so must you.

Most beginner infiltrators have difficulty determining whether a sound should be considered startling or not. A startling noise is defined by three characteristics: it is loud, highly proximate and follows a period of relative silence. It may not be easy to identify all the three characteristics fast enough to react accordingly. In his memoirs, infiltrator Zorn confessed that it took him over a year to learn not to shriek and pretend to panic every time he heard the sound of a cow bellowing in a distant meadow, so do not feel bad if you don't get it right from the start.

When assessing whether to interpret human speech as a startling sound, pay particular attention to the most ancient word in the human vocabulary: boo. On one of his first missions to Earth around 100,000 years ago, infiltrator Zorn made the first documented attempt of conveying a message to the leader of what at the time was one of the most progressive human tribes. Zorn's message was never properly documented (although it is believed to have regarded local space-craft parking opportunities), but the chieftain's response was logged in Zorn's report as "boo". This is believed to be the very first word humans ever used, and it is said to have remained the only word in human language for another two to three thousand years until the word "bah" was invented, carrying every meaning that the word "boo" hadn't yet covered. It wasn't until the invention of the third word, "hand-kerchief", that the word "boo" slowly started to go out of fashion, gradually giving up meaning after meaning to newly invented words. Of the few remaining meanings of the word "boo", one is to be considered a startling noise.

The appropriate manner of the responding to "boo" can be more or less freely selected from the general range of standard-looking scared responses we have described earlier. Shriek, jump, throw up your hands or slide your body away from the source of the "boo" – all as long as you do it immediately. If you fail to respond within three seconds you might just as well give it up altogether. An absent response to a "boo" would be a lot more human-like than a shrieking jump to the ceiling after a five second delay.

It also goes without saying that this manner of response should be reserved for this particular meaning of the word "boo". Jumping up and screaming in supposed terror when being sweet-talked to by your human spouse – or when undercover as a politician passing by an angry mob after having withdrawn housing subsidies for low-income humans – is considered poor undercover practice.

Being Alone in the Dark

Humans fear the dark. Most probably this fear is caused by their anticipation of accidentally bumping into things and hurting themselves due to their extremely poor night vision. To avoid this, humans intentionally paralyse their bodies, turn off their main brain functions and lay still throughout the darkest part of each day. Before doing so, humans position themselves on an elevated platform they call a "bed" and cover themselves with a thin sack of avian integument – possibly to avoid being detected by spiders or stepped upon by other humans fumbling around in the dark.

Having Your Human Body Seen by Other Humans Without Camouflage

Humans despise the sight of their own bodies and therefore panic if they are exposed to the sight of others. This fear somehow diminishes the closer humans are to water. In coastal areas you may find plenty of humans walking and lying about with their bodies almost entirely uncovered showing no signs of intimidation.

It is hard to establish exactly how close you need to

get to the water to not have to look frightened when not wearing clothes. The safest way to know is to look around you and examine other humans. If you find yourself being the only one standing naked in the street – immediately start squeezing out those eyes, screaming and covering your reproductive organs with the extremities of your frontal appendages. That should bring the situation closer to the state of normality.

~

How to Appear Stressed and Anxious

Stress and anxiety are hard to distinguish from each other, but the protocols for faking both of these emotions are the same.

The first protocol is to increase your movement speed a notch. That shouldn't be too difficult. The average natural movement speed of most sentient creatures in the universe is almost seven thousand times that of an average human, so a twenty percent increase should be both sufficient and pleasurable. Higher movement speeds may look suspicious.

Be careful not to accidentally switch to normal speed, because by the time you readjust, you will have created an illusion of you having teleported yourself from one spot to another in the blink of an eye. Such manoeuvres tend to arouse excessive human curiosity. Should that happen and you find yourself needing to adjust the speed back – be careful not to turn that switch back too fast, or you may accidentally turn it all the way down to plant speed. Infiltrator Zorn once made that mistake during his mediaeval infiltration mission. His accidental slip on the speed switch delayed the humans' Enlightenment project by almost a thousand years – a period modern humans now refer to as "The Dark Ages".

The second protocol of acting stressed is to simulate partial cognitive malfunction. Stress and anxiety have an arresting effect on human cognitive ability, resulting in overproduction of what is commonly known in the galaxy as "human error". It usually occurs when stressed humans try to save time by doing multiple things simultaneously.

Humans call this method multitasking.

It is a great method for species that are able to process multiple mental ques in parallel. For humans, on the other hand, it means increasing the total time spent doing things by adding two minutes of re-focusing time to every minute of everything they do.

It also means doing everything badly and constantly generating random undesirable events. Consider the following examples.

A common daytime behavioural pattern of a mentally stable human is to take the stairs down to the copy room (a cloning facility for slices of dead plants), clone a dead plant slice, bring both slices back up to the work desk, then take the stairs down a second time to pour a cup of coffee (water passed through pulverised fried plant corpses), then bring the cup up to the desk.

By comparison, the behavioural pattern of a stressed human would be to take the stairs down to the copy room, run to the coffee machine while cloning is in progress, pour a cup of hot coffee, bring most of it back to the copy room while leaving some on the office carpets and some on their own apparel, leave the cup by the copier, run back up to the work desk, realise (an hour later) that the original plant slice is still in the copier, take the stairs down to the copy room again, discover the cup of cold coffee that had mysteriously gone missing an hour ago, place it on the lid of the copier while using both hands to extract the jammed plant slice, then catapult the coffee across the office space by decisively lifting the copier's lid with the right hand while reaching underneath it with the left to extract the slice, release the lid back onto the left hand while following the coffee's trajectory with their gaze until it reaches the newly dry cleaned suit of a superior human, only to conclude the sequence with a solemn observation of the cup with the inscription "Employee of the Month" making gravity apparent to the head of the superior human's office cat.

It is a common myth that female humans are better at multitasking than male humans. Neither of them can really multitask, but females are slightly better at combining certain activities, while males are slightly better at combining others. For instance, females are more capable of conducting a coherent remote conversation while simultaneously shopping for human fuel and preventing their offspring from stealing insulin production stimulators. Males, on the other hand, are more capable of watching four different sports broadcasts at the same time, while simultaneously losing their ground vehicle keys and forgetting about their engagement anniversary.

Human error is hard to deliberately reproduce, as it makes absolutely no sense, follows no logic (hence the name) and often follows a sequence of reasonably sensible actions. There are, however, several methods of imitating it. One is called "Third Random" and is a rather simple rule of thumb where you deliberately randomise your every third action. It goes like this: perform two sensible actions consequently – and then conclude with a third action that is entirely random. For example:

- Pour the coffee (sensible action) – add milk (sensible action) – pour out the coffee (random action).
- Listen to a keynote speaker (sensible action) – pick up a pencil (sensible action) – draw a moustache on a photo inside a fashion magazine (random action).
- Clean your house – receive guests – tell them to keep their shoes on.
- See a pedestrian – step on the brakes – curse in front of children.
- Iron a shirt – put down the iron – burn down the house. (That last one may be in the twilight zone of effectiveness.)

Excessive magnitude of the random action can sometimes divert humans' attention too much from your main goal: making them believe that you are stressed. This was clearly demonstrated by infiltrator Zorn in what later became known as the Chernobyl event, but was initially Zorn's attempt at a Third Random sequence: open the front door – let the dog out – blow up a nuclear plant in Ukraine.

The third protocol of acting stressed is pretending not to hear parts of the things humans tell you. Here infiltrators commonly use a ten second rule. It goes like this: whenever a human starts speaking to you, look into the human's eyes and initiate a countdown starting at ten seconds. When the time is up, move your gaze away just a notch and fixate it on any object behind the talking human. Keep your eyes focused on it until the human starts calling your human name and waving at you. Look back at the human, apologise and repeat. Excusing yourself as being stressed should sound very credible after three to four repetitions. You will also see the speaking human showing anger, which is something you will need to learn as well.

~

Being Angry – When and How

Anger is a common mammal state of mind that often arises when the mammal finds itself in a situation of discomfort, like when a whale finds its blowhole stoppered by a buoy or when a dog encounters a human delivering paper messages to a neighbouring habitat. With humans, anger has a wider variety of causes than with most mammals. Here are the most common ones:

- Other humans not fully submitting to one's point of view
- Being misidentified as something one obviously isn't, such as a reproductive organ, a female dog or a pile of humanium
- Having the items in one's habitat rearranged in a more logical manner by another human
- Unmet expectations regarding the time span between the choosing of food and the feeding
- The discovery of a unilateral financial obligation following a poor on-land vehicle positioning choice
- Being reminded of the excessive obesity of one's female parent
- One's foot being used as a landing surface for heavy objects
- Being excluded from a mating session by one's regular mating partner (especially when another human is included)
- Untimely or unsolicited entertainment – particularly at the expense of someone who is terminally ill or a victim of some recent terrible atrocity

- Having parts of one's body removed without consent
- Being exposed to unpresentable illustrations of an admired individual or sacred deity
- Watching one's kin being murdered or one's habitat being set on fire
- Another human assuming one's desired seat at a feeding station while food is being acquired

When one of the above triggers is activated you should immediately exhibit anger. Humans typically express their anger in the following ways:

- Changing one's facial colour and pressing one's lips together harder than what is necessary for plain avoidance of infection
- Briefly but decisively ordering an undefined (and sometimes non-present) someone to engage in sexual intercourse
- Yelling about humanium
- Yelling about mating humanium
- A variety of suppressed screams, with the velocity being proportional to the magnitude of anger
- Employing surrounding objects to produce loud noises
- Destroying nearby objects and murdering nearby creatures

- Voting for psychopaths in general elections
- Ignoring questions and leaving when spoken to
- Performing completely random actions in an excessively careless manner, such as cleaning drinking vessels or stacking and rearranging objects on nearby surfaces. For this method to work it is very important to avoid all eye contact with the supposed object of anger and keep your facial muscles as relaxed as possible.

Not all of these methods of expression are equally optimal in each situation that demands anger expression, but you will learn which ones work best for you in time. Just try them out one by one and when you see humans either backing away or lashing out at you, then you know you got it right.

∾

Reflexes, Instincts and Compulsive Behaviours

Every once in a while, a human may act based on rational reasoning, but generally humans are programmed to act in accordance with a set of compulsive behaviours they like to call "instincts". Some of these made sense when evolution still applied to humans, while others seem to have been put in there for a joke.

Among the useful instincts is the compulsive urge to remove one's hand from the immediate reach of a crocodile's jaws or to stop breathing when under water. Among the less useful is the compulsive urge to express one's opinion in a matter where it clearly contradicts the opinion of one's counterpart to an extent that makes expressing it very unlikely to advance the expressor's social standing with the receiver. Although the life expectancy of humans who frequently fail to resist this urge is slightly lower than the average, the fact that murder is universally outlawed on Earth leaves little hope that complete peace will ever be established on this planet.

A similar compulsory behaviour is to point out spellings that do not conform to the most currently accepted grammar standards. Humans can sacrifice strong alliances and hours or days of their pitifully short lives for the sake of asserting that their understanding of the optimal sequence of characters in a word is one that best adheres to the prevalent linguistic norms of the language in question.

Most of the useless human compulsive behaviours are rather harmless. Nodding to repetitive sounds is one. If you repeat two phrases with the same number of syllables one after the other over and over while empha-sising the same syllable with consistent timing, humans will start nodding their heads to it for no apparent reason.

The same thing happens if you start banging on a hollow object with your hands at consistent intervals. At first we thought this was some sort of a clever way of keeping deaf humans updated on the sonic environment, but then our scientists discovered that the nodding only occurs when the intervals are shorter than one second, which led us to believe that this must be another compulsory behaviour with no apparent purpose.

Another compulsive behaviour that was once thought to be harmless is touching wood when hypothetically undesirable events are being mentioned. When infiltrator Zorn was working undercover as a beach lifeguard, he occasionally used this compulsive behaviour as a clever trick to get humans out of the water when needed. He would call out to the bathing humans the hypothetical possibility of a shark encounter, and as there was no wood for them to touch at that moment, the humans felt compelled to immediately head for the shore to find some. Zorn's report stated that for some human swimmers the urge to touch wood appeared to be so strong that they cried and screamed in frustration over not having any. Some even suffered heart attacks and drowned before they could reach land and satisfy their wood touching urge.

Zorn really enjoyed being a beach lifeguard.

Among the more dangerous compulsive behaviours is touching things when explicitly told not to. This is why a human nuclear weapon launch requires more red buttons to be pushed simultaneously than the number of fingers any single human body is equipped with. It is only a matter of time before enough humans with access to these buttons concede to the compulsive urge to push them simultaneously, thereby unleashing a nuclear apocalypse.

Another dangerous compulsive urge is the immediate need to burst out into laughter and wave one's limbs uncontrollably when being poked on the sides of one's waist or under one's feet. Never do this to a human driving the vehicle you are in. Also, avoid making sudden noises near a human that carries your teapot, as sudden noises seem to trigger a similar compulsive response with humans, only briefer and accompanied by a scream instead of laughter.

A related compulsive behaviour is to hold one's breath between hiccups. A hiccup is a curious behaviour in itself, where a human suddenly jerks their head upward, sucking a tiny burst of air into their throat only to immediately block its movement by contracting their throat muscles. The sound a human makes when doing this is one of the most prominent human ways of expressing their individuality. Since hiccups are uncontrollable and since humans despise not being in control, they regard hiccups as a menace and fight them bitterly by deliberately suffocating themselves.

Somewhere in the twilight zone between reflexes, instincts and compulsive behaviours resides a phenomenon humans call a "biological clock". It usually manifests itself in a human's consistency in deciding to go to bed early every evening and always ending up in bed at exactly 2 AM. With female humans it may also produce the side effect of sudden resentment towards all contraceptives, shortly followed by a manic obsession with the acquisition of cats. Since both of these biological clock manifestations tend to occur at a predictable point in time, they can be effectively used for telling the time of day or the age of a given human in the absence of a more advanced time measurement device – thereof the name.

Although most human survival instincts are actually useful, they are strongly biased in favour of imminent threats. Humans are terrified of things that kill them quickly, but adore things that kill them slowly. For instance, humans are generally terrified of bears, but fond of children. If you aggregate all the suffering an average human child inflicts on its parent and present it to an average human parent in the form of an imminent threat, the parent would much rather volunteer to be tied to a rampaging bear than endure parenthood. However, spreading this suffering evenly over the course of a human's adulthood up to their premature death not only makes it seem less unpleasant, but even desirable.

HIBERNATION AND DREAMS

Because the human brain has remarkably low bandwidth, it is unable to receive, sort and save data simultaneously. All data received is initially stored temporarily, while the sorting occurs during regular backlog refinement sessions known as "sleeping".

The most exciting parts of an average human's life usually occur during sleep. This is also when humans get to practise their roaring skills. Human children are hopelessly bad at roaring, but with years of sleeping practise their roar tends to improve – sometimes to a point where it begins to inflict permanent hearing damage. This is why ageing humans usually cannot hear very well, but are amazingly good roarers. In order to mitigate the impact of increasing roaring proficiency on hearing, evolution has provided human bodies with a protective in-ear hair growth, the luxuriousness of which is linearly proportional to a human's age.

The main excitement, however, happens during the memory sorting process. Before realising that there is no chance in the world that all the impressions from the day that has passed could fit in the human memory banks, the human brain stacks them all in an assorted pile of information to be taken care of later – as most humans do with most things. The pile includes both visual, sonar and other sensorial impressions, including remote associations and unrelated thoughts of large extinct reptiles, stockings that don't get torn or female bosoms.

Most of these memories are really not worth the storage space they take up. When there is way too little time left before the human wakes, the brain reluctantly gets back to work and starts scanning the pile in the hope that some pieces of data may have accidentally landed in the right order. As that almost never happens, the whole bunch is eventually discarded, with the exception of a piece or two left to create the impression of work having been done in case of external audit.

You know if a human has woken up before the impression pile has been discarded by their exhaustingly tiresome tales of completely improbable events, occasionally featuring the human being chased by large busty reptiles wearing remarkably durable stockings.

These ridiculous sequences of imagery are called "dreams". They have almost no tangible connection to reality, except for the very few that appear to display accurate events from the future. A famous human scientist called Martin Luther King, who evidently suffered from a rare sleepwalking condition, once had a dream when sleepwalking at a rally. To everyone's amazement, he was able to describe his dream in real time while having it, and it turned out to be a mostly accurate description of the state of events several decades into the future.

∼

HAPPINESS

Happiness is a human state of mind characterised by a severely reduced desire to cut one's own head off. It is most easily achieved through injecting certain chemicals into the human bloodstream, but is most commonly sought after using methods with significantly lower success rates.

Happiness is a rare state among humans. What is shared by most intelligent species as the primary purpose of living is generally as alien to humans as the idea of their home planet being a cube.

Humans are designed to be unhappy. Their intuitively perverted understanding of happiness is entirely rooted in desire. Humans always desire something: things, acknowledgement, other humans, ponies, terrain vehicles, being someone else, silence, having their rectum scratched – there is always something.

To make matters worse, they are programmed to desire the most that which they cannot have.

As a precaution against accidental happiness, humans are also equipped with a self-fuelled desire inflation mechanism. In the unlikely event of a human managing to acquire what they desire the most, they immediately begin desiring something even more unattainable. In order to ensure that this works even with the most unimaginative specimens, humans are equipped with a pathological urge to constantly compare themselves with everyone around them.

This terribly cruel design flaw was long believed to be a bug. However, according to a recovered log belonging to one of the original genetic designers, the design team had deliberately developed this feature at the last moment in a desperate attempt to speed up the pace of Earth heating, which was embarrassingly lagging behind schedule. The feature showed to be a great motivator for developing, building and consuming planetary resources without restraint. It allowed humans to progress into the industrial age and start building steam engines three hundred times sooner than the much more intelligent dolphins, who still spend most of their days catching waves and enjoying life with almost no tangible impact on the atmosphere temperature.

Humans can only feel happy for brief moments at rare occasions when they no longer feel compelled to compete with other humans. This almost exclusively happens under the influence of chemical substances or at the end of mating sessions – and much of it is presumably faked.

~

Zorn search party telepathic intercom transmission excerpt 3

Transmitted 2 hours and 11 minutes after dispatch.

Balbooza: [*I don't think this is working.*]
Gee: [*Relax, Balbooza. Just keep staring down into that flat hand-held device and walk calmly alongside me.*]
Balbooza: [*Everybody is staring at us.*]

Gee: [*They won't have anything to stare at if you act natural.*]

Balbooza: [*I think they can tell that I'm a chimpanzee.*]

Gee: [*Don't be ridiculous. How could they? You're wearing trousers, shoes, a shirt, a janitor's cap and a pair of sunglasses. What kind of chimpanzee wears that?*]

Balbooza: [*Maybe the front appendages are giving me away. I don't see any humans dragging theirs along the ground as they walk.*]

Gee: [*Just stretch your back a bit more.*]

Balbooza: [*Also, their faces are a lot flatter than mine.*]

Gee: [*Then don't pout your lips like that.*]

Balbooza: [*And I think they can see too much of the fur.*]

Gee: [*Well, I did try to shave you, but you were the one who opted out.*]

Balbooza: [*I wouldn't have if we could have done it with a razor instead of a walrus tusk.*]

Gee: [*Balbooza, you know we aren't allowed to bring blades on board of teleporter beams, and they don't seem to do a lot of shaving at this zoo. That walrus tusk was the best thing available, though I perfectly understand that being shaved by it may have felt slightly unpleasant.*]

Balbooza: [*It might have been less unpleasant had it not been attached to the walrus.*]

Gee: [*We'll take care of it as soon as we get out of here.*

Zorn clearly isn't at the zoo anymore, or else he would have approached us already.]

Balbooza: [*What is this device I am staring at anyway?*]

Gee: [*I don't know. But it's flat and it's hand-held. I saw a zookeeper clinging to it and tapping on it with his thumb while sitting in front of a screen that projected humans chasing some spherical object. Looked very human to me.*]

Balbooza: [*Can we at least walk a bit faster, so we can get out of sight sooner?*]

Gee: [*I wish I could, but this oxygen tank on my back is quite heavy, these plastic underwater goggles are blocking my vision and these huge flat rubber shoes are extremely impractical.*]

Balbooza: [*Doesn't it bother you that they are about three times the size of everyone else's shoes?*]

Gee: [*From what I have read, large human shoes are a sign of large feet, and for some reason human males with large feet are considered very respectable.*]

Balbooza: [*What makes you think you are a male?*]

Gee: [*What makes you think I am not?*]

Balbooza: [*Well, I have been observing the differences between the human sexes since we started walking, and you do not quite fit into the male pattern on at least three parameters.*]

Gee: [*Which ones?*]

Balbooza: [*Your hips are wider than your shoulders, you have made surprisingly few complaints about any pain between your legs considering how tight your*

rubber suit sits around your crotch, and you have two
large breasts popping out of that big hole you acciden-
tally made in the suit when trying to shave me with that
walrus tusk.]

Gee: [*Good point. Anyway, these are the only shoes I*
have, and human feet are extremely ill suited for
walking the planet's surface at this level of gravity, so
these will have to do for now. Come on, stop worrying
about everything! We look like perfectly normal
humans. If anything can give us away right now – it is
poor self-confidence. So cheer up and keep walking.
We'll be out of sight soon enough and will have plenty of
time to regroup and figure out our next steps in finding
Zorn.]

Chapter 4

Communicating with Humans

Most humans are completely devoid of any telepathic abilities. The species does, however, possess something that resembles a perverted form of telepathy. Humans call it "reading between the lines". It is a strange ability to hear and read things that were neither said, nor intended. The things heard in this way usually aren't random, but very much in line with the listener's own thoughts processed through the prism of their opinion about the speaker. If humans like you, you can say more or less anything and be sure that it will be well received. If they dislike you, their brains will selectively pick out parts of what you say and put them together into the most malicious sequence they can fit into the stereotype they have decided to apply to you. Keep your expectations of their conciliatory intentions low and be prepared to be best remembered for things you haven't said.

Overall, humans appear to respond differently to the same factual information depending on the manner of its conveyance and the identity of its carrier. You can get away with any sort of nonsense if you get them to like you first and say it like you mean it.

As if their lack of telepathy wasn't constraining enough, humans also have an extremely dysfunctional predictive ability. You will often notice them saying "be careful" or "watch it" seconds *after* you have accidentally bumped your head on a cabinet door or dropped a fragile item to the floor. In effect, humans neither know what you are thinking nor are able to predict what you mean to say, which is why communicating with humans requires a great deal of skill. Due to the aforementioned human handicaps, this skill must be constrained exclusively to sonic and visual communication by means of one of the yet remaining human languages.

~

The Substitute for Mind Reading

You must have noticed the awfully unpleasant sounds humans make when accompanied by other humans or when remotely disturbed by other humans through their most precious hand-held electronic device. These ghastly sounds, the awfulness of which has caused more than one alien infiltrator's mental breakdown, are called "speech" and are, unfortunately, this species' preferred method of transmitting sonic information.

Speech consists of pre-defined combinations of sounds humans call "words". Each word represents a thing, an action or a trait and is different in every human language. (Humans still haven't managed to agree on which language to speak, so they speak different ones.) This means that different humans will make a different sound for each word, and only those speaking the same language are able to understand them. The safest way you can address this unnecessary inconvenience is to learn all human languages. For a moderately intelligent species this should not take more than twenty minutes (although a human usually manages fewer than three in a lifetime), provided that you have all the data at hand.

However, exposing yourself to so many horrific sets of sounds may inflict irreparable damage to your processing units. We therefore advise you to learn a handful of larger languages that should cover most of your communication needs, and simply avoid humans who do not speak them.

Communicating through language has the convenient benefit of limiting your communication to one cue at a time, which is roughly what an average human brain is able to handle. Multiple simultaneous messages tend to make humans confused and unresponsive – especially the males.

Try not to get too attached to a language once you

have learned it. Human languages change so fast that even a couple of centuries-old writings can be utterly unintelligible to contemporary humans. Yet, due to one of the compulsive behaviours explained earlier, some humans will react furiously even to the slightest deviation from the linguistic norms of the most recent decade, and most will feel compelled to correct you. You must therefore choose your words and spelling based on which generation of humans you are speaking to and on the overall stupidity level of each specific human.

Even the richest human languages only have roughly half a million words, leaving over seven trillion things, traits and actions almost impossible to convey. This fixation on words has made humans oblivious to the mere existence of things they do not have a word for. With this in mind, it is hardly a surprise that out of all intelligent species on Earth, humans are the only one we still haven't been able to establish a productive diplomatic dialogue with.

 ~

Oral Conversation

Listening to humans speak is a pain. You will often feel tempted to seek refuge with ear plugs and revert to mind reading. Yet it is paramount to the success of your mission that you stay resilient and suffer the sound of the message you already know before responding, or else the humans may panic. If anything could be worse than a talking human – it would be a panicking human.

During your first interactions, you may feel uncertain about where to begin your conversation. Humans normally initiate dialogue with strangers by exchanging verbal descriptions of the current atmospheric conditions. We believe this to be a security measure devised to assess the sanity of the counterpart before exchanging any meaningful information. This measure also makes a rather convenient exercise for beginners. Just start off by stating which side of the average the current air temperature is by using a suitable adjective and displaying your approval or disapproval of the mentioned state of things. Approval should be displayed if the temperature is close to average, or slightly above, while deviating temperatures should be stated with disapproval. Unless you mix those up, the response will usually be a positive confirmation, enriched with a speculation on a more precise temperature measurement. At this point you may make a similar assessment of the previous day, and then of the past week, month or year. Once these obvious circumstances have been established without any noticeable protest, you can start turning the conversation into something at least remotely useful.

If your goal is to keep a human entertained and engaged in conversation until any useful information can be extracted from them, your best bet is to avoid talking about anything important. Our observations indicate that the subjects humans find most interesting are those that have the least impact on the life and well-being of humanity. You are far more likely to evoke human interest by verbally assessing the body wrapping of another human or the accuracy with which a certain human has placed an inflated spherical object within the boundaries of a rectangular drawing on the planet surface than by elaborating on potential improvements in nuclear technology or methods of preventing mass starvation. Remember that the human intellectual capacity likely amounts to only a tiny fraction of yours, so do not expect to learn anything substantial. It can be very frustrating to speak at a human's pace, but this is the only way they can have a chance of understanding you. If a human asks you how you are, know that it is a trick question. Do not disclose any details about your origin or anatomy. You can effectively neutralise the interrogator by briefly describing yourself as "well" and then asking the same question back.

If you are conversing with a human in a language you know and the human suddenly starts making monstrously repulsive sounds which do not make any sense to you – don't panic. Most probably, the human is laughing. Laughter is a sequence of vocally produced sounds that unique to every human and are therefore hard to recognise. It is often used as a sign of approval – or disapproval, mockery, mental fatigue, severe intoxication or as a response to having one's sides touched in an unsolicited manner or to seeing another human accidentally hurting themselves.

The variety of laughter-eliciting circumstances is so vast that it is usually of little use to try to establish the cause of laughter in every given instance. It is, however, very important not to allow the laughter to pass unrecognised. Typical newbie alien behaviour is to either ignore the laughter or to crouch in disgust and cover one's ears whenever laughter is elicited. Post-abduction surveys indicate that these behaviours make laughing humans very uneasy.

The optimal response to laughter is to laugh back. Many infiltrators find this challenging because every human's laughter is unique and it is almost impossible to establish what really defines a laugh. Judging by the multitude of available human laughter transcriptions, humans appear to be under the impression that their laughter simply constitutes a consequent repetition of the syllable "ha". However, infiltrator Zorn's multiple attempts at imitating genuine laughter by adhering to this belief were almost always perceived as mockery by laughing humans. Simply mimicking the laughter of a presently laughing human seems to produce the same undesirable effect. Your best chance at imitating genuine human laughter is by mimicking the laughter of a human who isn't currently present.

~

WRITTEN COMMUNICATION

In order to spare themselves from having to constantly endure each other speaking, humans have invented writing. Instead of making yet another awful sound for each piece of information they need to convey, writing allows humans to produce a sequence of visual symbols on a surface. Seeing these symbols makes the receiver imagine the aforementioned sound in their head and feel equally disturbed without actually hearing it. This is, of course, extremely inefficient, but you will soon learn that inefficiency is one of the defining traits of the human species. A human can spend hours composing, symbol by symbol, a message that would have taken minutes to convey by means of speech and seconds by means of telepathy.

One advantage of written communication is that it can remain in place with little or no additional energy spent. This makes it particularly convenient for making road or wall signs. Where a human otherwise would have had to stand all day at the side of the road yelling at passing vehicles to slow down, a sign with a speed limit inscription – although relatively useless compared to telepathic transmission – would drain a lot less energy from everyone involved.

∽

Figures of Speech

A classic infiltrator trap is when an unfamiliar human in the street asks them to spare some change. You would think that the most logical way of satisfying a request like this would be to alter your appearance or intended travel trajectory (the latter is, in fact, a rather commonly observed human response to unsolicited requests for change or the anticipation of such when seeing unfamiliar humans sitting idly along their path). However, doing so will not satisfy the needs of the human in question – even if no significant harm will be done either. It took infiltrator Zorn many alterations to realise that when phrased in this manner the requested change is meant to be applied to the asking human. It then took an even longer array of alterations applied to begging humans (very few of which have been well received by the askers) to discover the concept of figures of speech.

Figures of speech comprise an array of deliberate human speech distortions, such as purposefully using a word or a phrase wrong – often to describe something entirely unrelated. Why humans do this is still a mystery, but it is often believed to be a form of code, devised to conceal the true meaning of human conversations from possible infiltrators.

When trying to crack this code you should know that some words may have multiple figurative meanings, as is the case with the word "change". Its first figurative meaning was discovered by infiltrator Zorn during his undercover mission as a caretaker in a nursing home. Initially, this discovery was believed to be a great breakthrough in accurately responding to human change requests. However, Zorn's first attempt to apply the nursing home change procedure to a human asking for change proved that further research on the subject was required. Zorn's report from this incident provided valuable insights into the numerous challenges with applying sanitary procedures to a grown human in plain public sight. It also greatly extended Zorn's vocabulary with a whole range of new figures of speech.

Only much later it was discovered that humans asking for change are really asking for the financial means needed to achieve that change (even though the means received seem to very rarely be used for that purpose). To know if the meaning of change is figurative or not, pay close attention to the asking human's limbs. If the human reaches out their frontal appendage with the grabbing unit turned upwards – then the request is most likely a figure of speech. Please do not confuse this gesture with a popular human request known as a "Low Five". In his chronicles, infiltrator Zorn admitted that he still occasionally makes the mistake of hitting the palms of begging humans with his hand and placing coins into the hands of enthusiastic human co-workers looking for positive affirmation.

Human figures of speech are so numerous that a separate guide will have to be published in order to cover them all. In fact, it has been announced that infiltrator Zorn is authoring a volume of his own, consisting exclusively of figures of speech learned during unfortunate encounters with humans who lack a permanent habitat. Here we will provide a brief overview of human figures of speech which are the most hazardous ones to be ignorant about.

If you have been assigned a human partner, you will inevitably experience moments of mild friction with them. Unless duly addressed, such friction may develop into major conflict where your human suit may be damaged and your mission compromised. You can prevent such development by timely and accurate reading of figurative speech. If your human partner says that she (less frequently he) needs more space, you may find that immediately venturing off to colonise another sector of the galaxy will indeed help. The key words here are, however, not "space", but "immediately" and "off". Any verbal inquiries regarding the desired amount of space or its preferred location will only make matters worse.

Humans have a complicated relationship with the primary product of their metabolism (the one we call "humanium"). Although it clearly seems to be the main purpose of human existence, humans often use the various names they have for it as metaphors for the worst things they know. A rule of thumb is that whenever a human speaks of humanium, they most likely mean something else. Unless the human is standing next to a clearly visible pile of humanium, points at it and proudly proclaims that in the direction of the point there lies a pile of humanium, the meaning is almost certainly metaphorical.

This, however, is the easy part. It so happens that the numerous synonyms humans have for humanium (more numerous, in fact, than for any other known substance) have almost equally numerous metaphorical meanings. You must therefore pay close attention to the context.

If humanium is described as "good", then it is a metaphor for whatever the human is currently experiencing or consuming. This is the sort of context where the literal meaning of the word is usually the rarest. If a human tells you to mate with certain specific (although not obviously present) humanium, you may assume that what they are actually trying to say is that they are displeased with the current circumstances and are no longer willing to make any further effort to endure them. When a human points out in an accusatory manner that you aren't acquainted with some unspecified humanium, what they actually mean to say is that they are displeased with you providing information about a topic you are seemingly unfamiliar with.

Humans often use mating as a metaphor for displeasure. This is most confusing, since all evidence shows that most humans find mating quite pleasurable. Still, as an infiltrator, you are advised not to act on any human prompt that involves mating until you are absolutely sure that the human is not being metaphorical. If you ever see a human masturbating in public, it is most probably an undercover alien taking an unfriendly metaphor literally. Many of our infiltrators have been convicted of sexual assaults only because they couldn't tell a figure of speech from a call to action.

Overall, it is worth knowing that any figure of

speech that relates to mating is likely hostile. Our analysis of human hostile verbal metaphors indicates that humans utterly despise anuses and believe that mating is among the worst things that can happen to a human. Using such unfriendly figures of speech is called "cursing" and will be further explained in the next section.

~

SARCASM

When a human says something that appears to indicate an inadequate perception of reality, you should not immediately assume that the human is mentally defective and eject them through the airlock. It may be that the human is being sarcastic.

Sarcasm is a human way of being entertaining by saying things that contradict everything that makes any reasonable sense. As most humans are in the habit of regularly contradicting common sense without actually being sarcastic, sarcasm can be rather difficult to distinguish from mere stupidity.

If you need to establish whether something a human is saying is sarcasm or not, ask yourself: "Does this make any sense?". If the answer is "no", then ask yourself: "Am I speaking to a (by human standards) complete and utter idiot?" If the answer is still "no", then you can be reasonably sure that the human is being sarcastic. If it is a "yes" (as it will be with most humans) then – airlock. It does occasionally happen that complete and utter idiots are being sarcastic too, although their capability for both using and understanding sarcasm is usually severely arrested. Yet few of our operatives have ever regretted ejecting such subjects into space by mistake.

The basic idea of sarcasm is to pass a reasonable judgement by stating its obviously unreasonable opposite. Although it may sound simple enough, we normally advise our infiltrators against trying to use sarcasm on humans due to the high evacuation costs in case of failure. Infiltrator Zorn has empirically proven that using sarcasm in courtrooms can be very hazardous, especially when responding to questions like "Do you plead guilty?" At one point Zorn also discovered that sarcasm may complicate things when responding to questions about hypothetical possession of explosives during airport security checks. Not only did the incident cost Zorn a missed flight, the thorough examination of his luggage that followed also put the famous infiltrator in a very awkward position of having to pretend that his probing device was nothing but a very elaborate sex toy, and that the human children he had abducted and neatly packed into his suitcase were merely free riders trying to secretly hitchhike along without buying airline tickets. The least favourable context for sarcasm Zorn has ever encountered was when he was going undercover as one of the hostages during a bank robbery. The otherwise handy sarcastic human comeback phrase "What are you going to do? Shoot me?" backfired in the most disappointingly literal sense, ruining both a high quality human body suit and a highly sophisticated abduction scheme involving a helicopter-shaped flying saucer.

~

Body Language

Confined to a vocabulary that covers less than 0.01% of all the trillions of subtle aspects of life, it is not surprising that humans feel the need to supplement their speech with other forms of communication. They often do this by means of a certain set of gestures and expressions commonly known as "body language". Essentially, any body gesture or combination of facial muscle contractions that isn't a result of an epileptic seizure, a chemical substance reaction or conduction of electric current can be classified as an expression of body language. Understanding human body language can be vitally useful in maintaining your safety – especially with humans who have the habit of initiating hostile action without verbalising their hostility or their intent to resort prior to violence.

According to infiltrator Zorn's chronicles, humans almost never verbalise their intention to mate with someone or to re-distribute someone's wealth to their own advantage, however imminent and indisputable such intentions may be. These intentions are, on the other hand, usually quite identifiable by means of body language.

If a human points a weapon at you when asking for items currently in your possession, it is usually their way of informing you of the low probability of these items ever reappearing in your possession again. It is a common infiltrator mistake to interpret the gesture as a trade proposal and grab the weapon while handing over the requested items.

Similarly, if a human points a weapon at you while complimenting the appearance of your human host body, it is usually an invitation to a mating session where the inviting party is not prepared to take a "no" for an answer. Do not use this as an opportunity to practise generosity by handing over your human suit to the complimenting human as a gift. Instead, disarm the human and use this as an opportunity to get some quality probing done. Humans who are in the habit of offering unsolicited body intrusions to strangers surely wouldn't mind being subjected to one themselves.

When humans roll their eyeballs backwards while relaxing their jaws and allowing their cheeks to support the full weight of their chins – it usually means that they aren't fully enjoying the re-broadcast of important safety information you have kindly bestowed upon them. It could also mean that the voltage in the nerve system scanner you have plugged them into needs to be reduced.

Although the purpose of body language is to aid inter-human understanding where words are not enough, our observations suggest that human body language communication often contradicts the messages humans simultaneously express by words. A common observation is that very few of the humans who pronounce the phrase "I'm fine" actually behave as if they are. (It is generally very hard to find a fine human.) Similarly, the most common human use of the phrase "Are you happy now?" is registered in contexts where happiness is very unlikely to be found and is made by humans whose bodies exhibit very little genuine concern for the recipient's happiness.

The greatest discrepancies between body language and oral language are usually observed in mating behaviours. Whenever a human uses body language to convey a desire to couple with another human, it is almost always accompanied by an entirely unrelated verbal message, if any. Human males often complement their bodily coupling invitation with a verbal proposal to go out. Human females – usually after having accepted the prior proposal and then escorted by the male back to their habitat – use the verbal proposal to "come in" in the same manner.

While learning to understand what a human is trying to say by means of body language can be very helpful to your mission, it is even more vital to learn to distinguish body language from other body movements. When listening to a human talking, the most common rookie infiltrator mistake is to focus attention on the human's frontal appendages. When they talk, humans have the habit of moving their appendages in a manner that clearly demands attention and seems to have no other purpose than to convey some sort of message. The movements are usually semi-circular outward rotations of limb extremities that may leave you with the impression that the human is repeatedly weighing invisible blobs of goo. In the Mediterranean region of Earth the movement is often performed with pursed fingers and resembles playing with a yo-yo over one's own shoulder. There are some other variations of the movement, but their common denominator is that they mean absolutely nothing.

For a long time it was believed that humans use these movements to purposefully distract their listener from the information they are conveying verbally in order to conceal the abundant flaws in their reasoning. However, later experiments showed that the movements tend to intensify as the speaker's engagement with the subject increases. Humans who don't much care about the message they are conveying seldom make any movements at all and may not even look at the recipient when conveying it. By contrast, humans who deeply care about their own message are the most frequent cause of accidental property damage in their proximity.

Our scientists believe this to be the result of yet another defect in the human genome. It makes reading human body language immensely more complicated. You can address this issue by preventively asking a human who is about to start talking to you to hold an open tub of sulphuric acid for you.

This usually makes their pointless limb movements less volatile.

You don't need to learn all of the human body language by heart, but it does help to at least learn the key body signal of emerging trouble. This signal is a wrinkled forehead. Humans hate wrinkles, so if a human voluntarily creates wrinkles on their face, you can be sure that something isn't right. Deliberately wrinkled humans are trouble. When this happens, try to divert the human's attention to something they like, like a smartphone or a car accident. If none are available, poke them on the sides.

∽

Offensive Language

The human phenomenon of cursing was discovered by our linguists quite recently after an extensive study of thousands of unresolved galactic infiltrator support tickets. The tickets originated mainly from our orbital research labs, where abducted humans are often subjected to rather intrusive scientific examinations.

It is well known that most humans find this experience quite unpleasant.

Yet our researchers have repeatedly reported that instead of using their verbal skills to convey their approximate level of discomfort and propose more convenient methods of approach, the human subjects would often revert to making contradictory and inaccurate statements about the researcher's origin, anatomy and intellectual abilities. Some statements appeared entirely decoupled from reality.

Some human subjects would refer to the researchers as holes inhabited by donkeys. (A donkey is a terrestrial ungulate with an intellectual capacity quite similar to a human, but with a lot more determination. Our zoologists are unanimously certain that donkeys do not live in holes.) When prompted to relax their muscles to enable a smoother probe insertion, many humans would urge the researchers to go to a place which religious humans believe to be a citadel of eternal torture and suffering. There is no known record of anyone ever going to that place willingly and it was not clear how going there could possibly make a probe insertion easier.

Distressed human subjects also tended to make various proposals regarding different mating behaviours, many of which the researchers were expected to perform on their own. Some suggested that the researchers were in the habit of sucking certain terrestrial birds. Others would offer their own seemingly absent birds for sucking.

Cursing still remains largely unexplained as to its purpose. The cause of it is almost always dissatisfaction with the current state of affairs or with someone's behaviour, but our scientists have yet not been able to register a single occurrence when cursing would have led to any beneficial outcome for the cursing human.

In pursuit of better guidance for future infiltration

missions, infiltrator Zorn has conducted a multitude of experiments testing various possible responses to cursing. His conclusion was that the worst possible outcomes are usually achieved by conceding to any prompt embedded in the curse phrase. You should therefore never go to any uninviting places or suck on any animals only because a cursing human encourages you to. The advised course of action when cursed at is to ignore the behaviour altogether.

The distinction between cursing and other senseless human dribble rests upon the rather ambiguous human understanding that certain phrases are profane. Profanity is a human social construct which enables certain words, however harmless, to make humans feel awkward. Because what usually makes humans feel awkward follows no comprehensible logic, you will have to simply memorise some of the more generic patterns.

Generally, most of the words that describe objects extracted from the various openings in the human body, the organs through which these objects pass right before emerging into the world and the process of their production are considered profane. One exception to this is children. Words describing the organs through which children pass are considered profane, as well as the words describing the process of making children, but children themselves are perfectly safe to mention at a dinner party.

Beware that this exception holds only for children whose father is known.

If a human inaccurately describes you with a phrase which you know is profane, or if the human urges you to engage in a behaviour that humans consider profane, it is something humans call an "insult". It is important to know that the inaccuracy of a statement meant as an insult is deliberate. It is therefore fruitless to try to explain to the human that their information is inaccurate and that you aren't at all the fragment of organic matter the human is mistaking you for. The expected course of action here is to get offended.

Being offended is one of the most typical human behaviours, which has grown increasingly fashionable in the recent decades. Offending someone used to be a human art form where verbal skills could be used to force a target human to experience negative emotions. With time, the array of phrases capable of producing this effect has multiplied exponentially to a point where offending humans no longer requires any skill at all.

There is, therefore, no point in diving too deep into the mechanics of offending humans. The data from our most recent infiltrator feedback survey confirm that offending a human is one of the easiest things one can do. All that's required is for you to say or write something a human does not like hearing or reading which, depending on the day of the week, the human's current hormonal balance and the compounded outcome of the human's previous life choices, could be virtually anything.

If you happen to say something offensive to a

human without intending to, you can easily remedy the situation by adding the safeword "no offence" afterwards. Whatever it is you just said will supposedly immediately stop being offensive – at least judging by our observations of how this phrase is commonly used.

While offending humans is easy, *being* offended (or acting it) may require some skill. It is something you will need to do a lot during your infiltration mission, especially if your human host body was manufactured after 1980 AD.

However strong the trend of increasing propensity to be offended may have been in the recent decades, humanity has not yet evolved to a level where a hundred percent of everything said and done can be accepted as a legitimate cause for feeling offended. It will, therefore, take some effort to identify the offensiveness in many things you hear and read.

An insult, as described above, is always offensive, unless it is meant as a joke, in which case it is only offensive if the non-flattering description of you happens to be accurate, like when jokingly calling someone diagnosed with a mental condition a moron for being slow. In the past, accuracy was something that distinguished insults from inconvenient truths, but in the latest stages of its evolution humanity has developed the ability to be offended by truth as well.

Regardless of whether it is true or not, most commonly humans will get offended when you attribute them any of the following characteristics:

- having a subnormal mental ability
- having a low level of physical attractiveness
- having a strong self-preservation instinct
- having excessive deposits of fat inside one's body
- being in the habit of mating with one's parent
- being short in size
- favouring a specific degree of skin pigmentation over others
- being a genital
- being a human of the opposite sex (technically, this means that being a human of any sex is an undesirable trait)
- being in the habit of providing deliberately inaccurate information
- being a small hen
- being a professional entertainer with a painted face and an orange wig
- lacking the ability to entertain other humans
- having existed longer than most humans
- having a propensity for sexual behaviours with low fertilisation probability
- lacking the ability to engage in sexual behaviours

This is, however, only the tip of the iceberg. The remaining 180 trillion list items will be published in a separate volume called "180 Trillion Things That

Offend Humans", which our team of humanologists is expected to make available for purchase no later than 3043 AD, with subsequent version updates needing to be published every two weeks and a new edition titled "190 Trillion Things That Offend Humans" projected to be ready for release the year after.

At this point you are probably wondering how humans appear when they act offended. The standard human way of responding to offence has developed greatly over the years. In the earlier days the expected manner of conduct would be to grab any available heavy object and strike the offending human's head with it multiple times until no further offence can physically be made. At a certain point in history, human males invented a new method of handling offence called a "duel", where both the offended and the offender would honourably agree to share a fifty percent chance of immediate death. More sophisticated methods have evolved more recently, of which some are still in use and may at times be too subtle to distinguish.

For instance, if a human asks you what your problem is, don't mistake it for sympathetic curiosity and begin to elaborate on all the hardships of life. Pretend that you have none and move away slowly. Another common human method of responding to offence is called "silent treatment". The way it usually unfolds is that the presumably offended human suddenly stops being annoying and leaves you alone. You may often feel tempted to offend humans only for the sake of receiving this treatment, but remember that offended humans are harder to extract intelligence from.

The human state of being offended can be easily removed by making the human believe that whatever it was you said or did to offend them actually made *you* feel bad. Nothing cheers a human up better than seeing another human hurt. The more you exaggerate how bad you feel, the sooner the offence will pass. Don't bother explaining in what way you feel bad. They will not care if it's nausea or diarrhoea – they'll just be happy enough knowing that you are suffering. Similarly, whenever a supposedly offending human indicates that they are in pain or sorry, you may stop acting offended.

This applies to almost all types of offence except for the one humans consider to be the very worst of them – expressing an unpopular opinion.

You can tell if an opinion is unpopular by anonymously posting it on a human social network and counting the number of insults you receive in response. The most human way of addressing an unpopular opinion is to insult its holder. You may gain additional bonus points if you reach out to other humans on the social network and encourage them to apply various verbal penalties to the holder of an unpopular opinion or plead to the social network itself to make the holder of the unpopular opinion less visible to other humans. Doing so is called *cancelling*, and is a common human method of trying to ensure that mainstream opinions remain mainstream forever. It usually works quite well until the number of cancelled humans begins to exceed the number of popular opinion holders, at which point the two tend to swap roles – usually accompanied by shorter intermezzos of mass violence and genocide.

Reacting to Irrational Behaviours

You will notice that much of the human behaviour you encounter does not fit into any logical algorithm. For example, a human may display signs of aggression after releasing a heavy object onto their lower limb, but will display signs of joy when the air pressure in another human's gastrointestinal tract is promptly lowered. These puzzling creatures may exhibit great distress when another human describes them as a piece of humanium or a rectum opening, even though the profound inaccuracy of such statements should seem unambiguously apparent even to the least intelligent mammals. Some humans tend to make loud sounds and move erratically when events unexpectedly turn to their advantage, and when the opposite occurs, they may do the same, but in a slightly different manner and with the occasional additional flavour of violent hair removal.

It is important not to lose your grip and panic when observing such seemingly inexplicable behaviours. It took infiltrator Zorn a great deal of practice before he finally learned not to blast humans into vapour with his chromosome dissolver every time they tried to cage him with their limbs in what he later learned were sudden expressions of affection provoked by his failure to be discrete when sneaking out their children out of their burning habitat for research purposes. It is due to these incidents that it has later become standard abduction practice to always sedate humans before setting their habitat on fire.

Fortunately, for most humans these deviating behaviours follow a certain pattern, which allows a diligent student of human behaviour to prepare an adequate response to each behaviour without raising too much suspicion. We will now go through the most common irrational behaviours and suggest a fitting course of action for each.

The most common human irrational behaviour is laughing. As explained earlier, laughter manifests itself as a sequence of rather unpleasant vocal sounds, produced by means of involuntary bursts of air emitted from the human's lungs and accompanied by facial muscle contraction. Fortunately, this behaviour is usually short-lived. Prolonged intensive laughter ultimately produces a lethal outcome. You may at some point need to use this to neutralise a human when unarmed. To do so, you must learn how to make humans laugh.

The easiest method is to repeatedly poke the human on the sides with your fingertips. If you manage to keep poking for at least two minutes without relief, death by suffocation is guaranteed (especially if the human's limbs are cuffed to metallic bars during the poking). If this is not possible (for example, if you are wearing a defective human body that has no hands, or if you need to quickly kill a human with laughter while you are performing a solo piano concert and are concerned about getting poor audience reviews), consider being funny.

Being funny comprises a diverse array of behaviours that range from purposefully hurting yourself through unreasonably poor limb coordination to making false claims about relatable issues. One of the simplest ways of being funny is to lie about a highly shocking circumstance, give the deceived humans a little time to process the information and then reveal that the information was untrue. Laughter usually comes right after, occasionally accompanied by a severe beating. To avoid the latter, substitute the word "lie" when admitting that you lied with the word "kid". Calling lying "kidding" somehow makes it a lot more acceptable to humans.

The processing time is crucial too. Admitting the lie immediately will not allow the laughter to properly develop, but giving the human enough time to be able to act on the received information may both decrease the intensity of the subsequent laughter and increase the severity of the beating that follows. If you tell a human that a local pizza restaurant holds human children captive in its basement in order to use them for cultist orgies, do not wait until the human has stormed the restaurant and killed its staff with a rifle until you tell him that it was all a lie designed to make him laugh.

Infiltrator Zorn once deliberately gave a famous Italian sailor with a strong curry craving wrong directions and allowed the man to sail off before he had the chance to reveal the truth. Following Zorn's directions, the sailor discovered a place that should have been left untouched, and that has ultimately led to an entirely different and less controllable world order (and to humans ruining a perfectly new doormat outside of our underground Lunar observation base by sticking a flag pole into it).

Another way of being funny is to speak of things humans normally avoid speaking about, such as mating, defecation or obesity. Why it makes humans laugh is almost as big a mystery as why humans avoid speaking about these things. Emphasising common behavioural differences between humans of different sexes is also a great way to provoke laughter, which is, oddly, something these differences never seem to provoke when they occur in real life.

A less sophisticated method of making humans laugh is to use clowns. A clown is a human whose appearance and behaviour amplifies the worst characteristics of a human. Clowns use a lot more makeup, are even more ridiculously dressed, are even louder, less coordinated and make less sense than even the least developed humans. Having a clown with you at all times is a useful habit if you want to be able to provoke laughter whenever it is needed. It does, however, have an adverse effect on stealth.

Overall, humans tend to laugh when seeing or hearing about other humans doing something ridiculous. By our standards, that would incorporate more or less everything humans do, but to humans "ridiculous" means something that humans do rarely and do not understand the purpose of, like pretending to sound like another human or being hit on the head with a heavy object. An odd point to note is that the same ridiculous behaviour may not be perceived as funny at all if it somehow relates to a vulnerable type of human, such as a human who is very young, very old, malfunctioning or dead. Dead humans aren't really vulnerable, but are treated similarly. However funny you make a dead human, most humans will not laugh, and some may even lash at you. So if your clown grows old or dies – which is a common habit among all clowns – dispose of it immediately. There is very little you can do with a dead clown that will make humans laugh. Infiltrator Zorn has experimented with over a hundred different tricks with his dead clown before real-ising this, having registered that all the children's parties he and his dead clown had visited appeared to be equally unappreciative of his efforts. Zorn's further attempts to lighten the mood of the parties by ridiculing the upset human children for not laughing at a dressed-up decom-posing corpse provided the useful insight that trauma-tised children are too a sub-stratum which is incapable of eliciting human laughter by behaving ridiculously.

It has been noticed that humans sometimes deliberately imitate laughing when another human is trying to be funny without much success. This only applies if the latter human is of a higher social stratum than the human pretending to laugh. Few humans ever bother to adapt their behaviour to humans of a lower social stratum, except when crossing the road in order to avoid awkward confrontations with beggars and charity fundraisers when low on currency.

One last thing about laughing: humans appear to attribute a great deal of importance to the order of laughter. To be the first one to laugh is something that seems to make humans uncomfortable, while being the last one to laugh gives humans great satisfaction. Therefore, if you want humans to be positively predisposed to you – always laugh early, but only after others have done so. Being the only one laughing in a room full of humans will make them perceive you as awkward, unless you are going undercover as an evil villain, in which case it would be perfectly natural, as evil humans are known to be very easily amused – even when things do not go their way. If you happen to have misinterpreted the mood and begun laughing before realising that none of the surrounding humans intends to join you – try poking them on the sides with your fingertips.

Another common irrational behaviour is crying. It too consists of a deeply disturbing mix of sounds and muscular contractions, but involves a much more intensive body liquid expulsion than laughing. Humans generally do not enjoy crying (although some deliberately acquire tickets to films that predictably lead them to it) and will be grateful for any help with ending this behaviour. Commanding them to stop usually doesn't help, so some special efforts need to be made in order to make the human reassess their need to cry. Such efforts go under the group name "comforting".

The most commonly observed comforting method is to tap the crying human on the shoulder with the flat side of the grabbing unit on your frontal appendage and mention an ambiguous direction twice, followed by an occasional repetition. However, our observations show no indication of any positive impact from this behaviour.

Another comforting method that is as common as it is useless is trying to impress the crying human with the gravity of other humans' suffering. It is likely meant as a distraction, but it tends to have quite the opposite effect, the intensity of which grows ever stronger the more expressly the suffering of other humans is presented.

A third common (and entirely useless) comforting method is to question the severity of the circumstance that led the human to cry. But this should only be used in certain circumstances. For instance, if the human is crying because their close relative has died, it is of little use to point out what an awful and smelly creature the relative was and how much space has now been freed up in the crying human's habitat.

It is also quite useless to try to outweigh the

human's crying with laughter. Infiltrator Zorn has tried this many times at funerals, and it just never seems to lift the prevalently depressing mood, regardless of how loudly you laugh.

Before comforting a human, always make sure that they are really crying. All three components of crying (eerie sounds, muscular contractions, liquid expulsion) seem to vary greatly between individuals, which makes crying very hard to distinguish from other irrational behaviours, such as laughing. You must carefully assess the character of each component, and the presence of the others, before you can be sure that the human is indeed crying.

The liquid expulsion is the easiest one to assess. All you need to check is that the liquid is expelled from the eyes, and not from any other body part. Make sure that you know where human eyes are, or else you may get locked up for public disturbance and harassment, as was infiltrator Zorn during one of his earliest missions after having been caught comforting strangers in a public restroom during his first mission to Earth, to which he had been assigned despite miserably failing his human anatomy exam.

Muscular contraction is a less evident component of crying. The contractions can be seen on the human's face in the form of the most repulsive facial expression a human can possibly make. Everything that can go wrong with a human face usually goes wrong when a human cries. When you see the level of attractiveness of a familiar human face suddenly drop from above average to nauseatingly hideous, without any prior exposure to sulphuric acid or a heated iron, the human is likely beginning to cry. If you ever need something you can use against a vain human for extortion purposes, taking a picture of them crying would be it. Non-facial muscles may contract too on crying humans, but there is no safe way of really telling what is going on if you cannot see the face. Humans contracting their biceps or thighs are usually not crying, so comforting them may not produce the desired effect.

The sound component is the least predictable one. Crying humans usually emit sounds that resemble the natural noises of various other mammals during mating rituals. These sounds are sometimes so similar to human laughter that you may feel encouraged to laugh as a response. Making that mistake will considerably complicate your ability to handle the situation in a manner that will ensure the human's future coop-eration.

If component analysis does not provide you with enough confidence, try examining the context of the behaviour. Crying usually occurs in conjunction with an event or circumstance that the human finds strongly undesirable, such as being subjected to intrusive research or having learned about the death of a geneti-cally related human. Humans have a strong preference against other humans with similar genetic code dying. If a dead relative is located next to the human who exhibits any of the aforementioned behaviours, then the human is most likely crying. Always look for dead humans in the proximity of a human that appears to be crying in order to be sure that they aren't laughing.

~

Adjusting for Personality

Once you have absorbed all the contradictory knowledge laid out above, prepare yourself for an additional layer of complexity. All aforementioned behaviours and tricks should be adjusted in accordance with a dimension that affects how every single human behaves in every given situation. This dimension is called "personality" and is a form of deviation from common sense that is exclusively attributable to one single individual.

Having a lot of personality makes a human less predictable (and usually annoyingly loud). Strangely, it also appears to make the same human more attractive to other humans. Before applying any of the mechanisms described above, it is crucial that you map the personality of the human first and adjust your methods accordingly.

A human personality has many layers and sub-dimensions. A simple example is a binary division of humans into optimists and pessimists. Optimistic humans are inherently ignorant about the evident hopelessness of their situation and are always in denial of the severity of their failures. Pessimistic humans are usually right about things, which makes them intolerably depressing and always makes one wonder why they are still alive, sometimes to a point that makes it hard not to assist them in correcting this obvious error of evolution.

You can easily tell the difference between pessimists and optimists during abduction. Optimists are the ones taking selfies and making notes for posts they will make on social media once they have mobile coverage again. Pessimists are the ones with lubricant in place already before abduction.

Another popular human personality dimension is the introversion-extraversion scale. Extroverted humans represent everything humans are generally known and despised for. Everything they say and do is a variation of "I am human! Hate me and rejoice that I will soon perish as a result of a cataclysmic event my race is solely and unequivocally responsible for." Introverted humans regard other humans roughly in the same resentful way as any other sane intelligent creature would and behave as if they are genuinely ashamed of who they are. Because of this they are sometimes easily confused with alien infiltrators and therefore seldom abducted.

The ways in which humans like to classify their personalities are abundant, but none of them is as accurate as that which determines a human's personality based exclusively on Earth's position relative to its sun at the moment of each human's first emergence from another human's most private body part. Although many humans still believe their personality traits to be a product derived by mixing two sets of genes, there is overwhelming evidence that all genes of a human embryo are, in fact, automatically altered between twelve distinct combinations as Earth makes its way along its solar orbit. Much like in a game of roulette, the final combination is locked depending on which of the twelve sectors of the orbit Earth is in when the human embryo decides it has had enough placenta and needs some fresh air. This explains why all humans you meet who are born in the same month have the exact same personality.

∽

Zorn search party telepathic intercom transmission excerpt 4

Transmitted 3 hours and 44 minutes after dispatch.

Balbooza: [*Gee, are you registering this noise?*]
Gee: [*Yes, I can hear you.*]
Balbooza: [*I am talking about that sonic noise droning in from behind that street corner.*]
Gee: [*Oh, that. Must be another accurate placement of an inflated sphere within a frame. Use your laser pulse spatial scanner to investigate the source. Is it coming from a bar?*]
Balbooza: [*No, I believe it is coming from human throats.*]

Gee: [*Yes, but are the throats in a bar?*]

Balbooza: [*How can throats be in a bar? I can see how a bar can be inserted into a human throat, but the other way around...*]

Gee: [*Balbooza, a bar is... Oh, never mind. Just read that two-pager please whenever you find the time. Are the humans producing the noise mostly bald males?*]

Balbooza: [*Indeed, they are. How did you know?*]

Gee: [*It's in the manual. Bald human males gathered in bars make loud noises when someone on an electronic screen places an inflated sphere where they think it should or should not be.*]

Balbooza: [*Well, these humans are not inside any bar. They are moving along the street in a large group and carrying bars with large rectangular plates attached at the top with things written on them.*]

Gee: [*Like what?*]

Balbooza: [*Well, there is one that says "We are full." Have you got any idea what that might mean?*]

Gee: [*It usually means that the humans are sufficiently fuelled up. They must have left the bar just now. Fuelling commonly takes place at bars. Not sure why they would want to go through so much trouble only to manifest a piece of information this insignificant... But then we are talking about a species that regularly posts images of their fuel on electronic social media for others to admire, so perhaps we shouldn't be too surprised.*]

Balbooza: [*Another one says, "Keep out."*]

Gee: [*Interesting. They must be so full that they believe themselves to be a hazard to others. I cannot recall* *human fuel being explosive. It does, however, tend to be quite unpleasant when emitted back out from the human body's various openings. Perhaps they are just being considerate, knowing that they may not be able to contain the fuel they have just filled themselves with. What else is there?]*

Balbooza: *["Veterans before immigrants."]*

Gee: *[That is probably just an instruction regarding their intended order of procession. What else?]*

Balbooza: *["Go home."]*

Gee: *[This one is clear enough, but I wonder whom it is addressed to...]*

Balbooza: *[There is another one that is more specific: "Illegal aliens, go home."]*

Gee: *[What?? They are not supposed to know! Are you sure that is what it says?]*

Balbooza: *[Positive. Gee, I am not fully au fait on the legal red tape – and I am not assuming that you are either – but just in case you happen to know... Are we illegal aliens?]*

Gee: *[Well, Balbooza, I do happen to know this much: all terrestrial dry land that is even remotely habitable is subjected to human migration law. The law varies from country to country, but one thing they all have in common is that in order to legally enter the airspace of any jurisdiction you must be in the possession of a passport issued by a country which is formally recognised in this jurisdiction. Do you have a passport?]*

Balbooza: *[What is a passport?]*

Gee: *[You would have known if you had had one, but to*

have one you must be a resident of a country, which you
are not, because countries are a construct that only exists
in the heads of humans. It wouldn't have been of much
help if you were, however, because there is yet no human
jurisdiction that recognises a country that isn't presently
located on Earth. Thus, technically, there is no way
anyone from any other planet can legally enter the
airspace of any part of Earth's dry land except Antarc-
tica, where even humans are reluctant to go – unless
effectively misled about the real reason behind Earth's
rising sea levels being anything other than Zorn's artifi-
cial planetary core inflation project.]

Balbooza: *[So that is a "Yes" then?]*

Gee: *[Well, if you are so firmly determined to establish*
this fact beyond all reasonable doubt, here are some
control questions. Have you submitted a visa applica-
tion form at the embassy of any human country on your
planet before coming here?]

Balbooza: *[I am not sure what a visa is, but I feel*
quite sure that I haven't.]

Gee: *[Do you have a visa stamp in your non-existent*
passport stating its date of issue and the period during
which you are allowed to enter a certain human
country?]

Balbooza: *[No.]*

Gee: *[When entering Earth's atmosphere, did you pass*
a passport control where a grumpy human immigration
officer compared your image in the passport with your
actual appearance enough times for you to age beyond
recognition or morph into a different creature in the

process, then asked you about the purpose of your visit and the details of your terrestrial accommodation only to wish you a pleasant stay in the most insincere of ways?]

Balbooza: *[Hmm... Not that I can recall.]*

Gee: *[Then you can be positively sure that you are as illegal an alien as almost one out of ten inhabitants of the human state of California, and so am I. Knowing that, I am quite disturbed by the message on that placard which you just read. Let us try to learn more. What do the other ones say?]*

Balbooza: *[There is one that says, "Stop the invasion".]*

Gee: *[Well, that is not good at all. Clearly our plans seem to have been compromised. There must be a leak. Or a mole. This is most serious, Balbooza.]*

Balbooza: *[Maybe this has something to do with Zorn's disappearance.]*

Gee: *[Let us not rush to conclusions. Perhaps they are acting on pure speculation and have no idea what our purposes are.]*

Balbooza: *[There is one that says, "You will not replace us".]*

Gee: *[So they do know our purpose. Well, this is a clear code red. We must report to the mothership immediately. What a terrible waste... Centuries of planning and scheming flushed down the drain. I expect more than one agency big shot gets fired or is subjected to a collusion investigation before we hit home base. How could this possibly have happened...?]*

Balbooza: *[Do you suppose that we should perhaps*

report to the mothership from elsewhere? These bald
humans are very close now and I fear that they might be
able to tell that I am an illegal alien.]

Gee: [*There is no time to relocate. We must report
immediately. Don't panic, Balbooza. You are wearing a
primate body, human clothes and are almost perfectly
shaven, so there really is nothing that could possibly give
you away as an illegal alien. Just keep your excessively
long frontal appendages folded and try to act as local as
you can.*]

Balbooza: [*I am not sure this will work.*]

Gee: [*Of course it will. Here, put this large scarf over
your head. I have seen some female humans wearing
these all over their bodies. You could hardly see what
species they were through that thin slit around their eyes.
Make sure to wrap yourself properly and you'll be
perfectly safe.*]

Balbooza: [*Could you try to distract them while I'm
putting it on?*]

Gee: [*Of course.*] Greetings, fellow homos! What a
cheerful and gay parade you are conducting! May I ask,
why do you prefer having the immigrants in the rear,
and not the veterans?

Chapter 5

Human Social Codes

Humans are a very considerate species. Most of them adapt their whole lives to what they believe that other humans expect of them – and humans expect quite a lot of each other. Most of these expectations are so hard to crack that humans call them "codes". "Social codes", to be precise, but since humans don't really have any antisocial codes, we will simply be sticking to "codes". Such codes are often dictated by something humans call "tradition". A tradition is a set of mostly irrational choices a human is expected to make throughout life in order to be spared from the one thing humans fear the most: rejection.

When you observe humans behaving in a coordinated manner that makes absolutely no rational sense, the explanation is usually tradition. Humans engage in traditional behaviours because they want to feel included – and because it is a far easier way of avoiding rejection than being useful.

Disregarding social codes may occasionally help you win presidential elections, but will otherwise more often than not alienate you from humans and complicate your infiltration mission. It is therefore of paramount importance that you avoid acting out of common sense when dealing with humans. Instead, follow as many codes and traditions as you can remember, and engage in every ritual you can. In this chapter we will go through the most typical ones.

∿

Compulsive Wrapping

It was mentioned earlier that humans have a strong habit of wrapping themselves in fabric materials at all times when they are out and about the planet's surface. When we first started observing this behaviour, it was assumed to be a way to compensate for the inherent human lack of fur during cold weather. Once it became apparent that the wretched creatures keep their bodies wrapped even when subjected to high atmospheric temperatures, it was instead assumed that the wrapping must be a form of camouflage. Their persistence in camouflaging themselves in outfits that bear little to no resemblance to their surroundings soon made the human species known as the second worst camoufleur in the universe after the ostrich. Unlike the ostrich, however, human camouflage seemed to work remarkably well on other humans. Numerous observations of crowded city environments showed that hundreds of wrapped humans were constantly passing each other by at a very close distance without ever seeming to notice one another – all until their wrapping was suddenly removed.

Today we know that human wrapping is a compulsive behaviour stemming from the contempt humans feel towards their own bodies. Having their body wrapped in various layers at all times has become such a prevalent part of human existence that they even have a word – multiple words, in fact – for *not* being wrapped, with "nude" and "naked" being the most frequently used. These creatures appear to absolutely detest the sight of other humans unwrapped (a sentiment somewhat understandable, considering what a nauseatingly hideous species we are dealing with). In fact, as a human, simply being seen looking like yourself can be punishable by law in many parts of the planet.

Curiously, a very small patch of cloth can make the whole difference between what humans consider to be scandalous nudity and perfectly normal beachwear. After a series of experiments, where a small patch of cloth has been placed over various parts of the human body before the body was released into a human crowd under observation, our scientists concluded that nudity to humans is actually not about the lack of wrapping, but about the ease with which they can observe each other's genitals.

Given the earlier established human fear of genitals, the human fear of nudity should appear understandable. What has been less obvious is why only one in two humans ceased to be perceived as naked once their genitals were covered up. To investigate this discrepancy, further experiments were conducted where small patches of cloth were randomly placed on different remaining uncovered parts of the human subject's body while the genitals remained covered at all times. The procedure was applied to thousands of human subjects. These were then randomly presented to human focus groups who were asked to assess each subject's nakedness. The experiment showed surprising results. The nakedness perception ratio firmly dropped from half to zero for all subjects whose both nipples were covered. Infiltrator Zorn, who led the experiment, concluded that the only rational explanation to this is that the human genome must contain one chromosome pair which is specifically responsible for whether or not a human is born with a phobia of nipples – with both combinations being equally probable.

Should you ever be accidentally exposed to another human when naked, the normal procedure is to emit a loud sound (preferably through the mouth), grab whatever object is close at hand and use that object to cover your reproductive organs and nipples. If the object is unsuitable for providing effective cover (for example, if it is an anvil, a two-handed sword or a desert snake), plan B would be to throw that object at the intruding human. This should make it very clear that your nudity was unintentional and should not be considered a criminal offence.

Overall, as your goal is to blend in seamlessly among humans, always wearing the authentically looking human suit all undercover agents are provided with (and not one of those cheap party costumes from Uranian discount stores you might wear on Galactic Monsters Day) is not enough. You will need a suit on top of the human suit. Moreover, in order to remain uncompromised for more than a week, you will need more than one.

Overexposure to close-up imagery of humans acquired by our Lunar observation post in the 1960s has spawned a misconception among first-timers heading for Earth that the most common human outfit is a pressure suit. Nothing can be further away from the truth. In fact, one of the most certain ways of getting compromised as an alien on Earth is to show up in a pressure suit. Don't do it. It has been tried before. Besides, according to infiltrator Zorn's primaeval era chronicles, pressure suits severely arrest one's movement speed and agility when escaping large terrestrial predators.

You will blend in a lot better if you wrap your body into multiple layers of fabric material. Be aware, however, that your choice of materials and how you combine them will be a matter of great concern for virtually every human you meet.

Our first suspicions of humans' unhealthy fascination with other's wrappings began when some human archaeologists made an unannounced visit into our teleportation chamber at the bottom floor of one of our seven pyramidal fusion power plants in Egypt. (We built these plants some six thousand years ago in the hope that they would provide enough energy to sustain the human population growth for the upcoming millennia. It took humans two centuries and a dozen wars to completely forget how to use them, but at least they have finally stopped putting their dead leaders under them.) The newly arrived infiltrator Zorn, whose luggage had been mistakenly teleported to Uranus, where it had to wait until Uranus had made another rotation around its sun and was inside Earth's teleportation range again, was only wearing his human suit.

Being an experienced infiltrator, Zorn knew how badly humans reacted to seeing other humans without any wrapping. In order to spare the approaching archaeologists the unpleasant experience of seeing another human body, Zorn quickly wrapped himself in some old rags he found in a gilded human-shaped piñata some human hooligan had dumped right in front of the teleporter. At a careful pace, he walked towards the glimmering torchlight, carried by the expedition leader at the far end of the catacomb, feeling his way through the dark with his outstretched frontal appendages.

The few survivors of the stampede that followed in the narrow stone tunnels leading out of the pyramid made it abundantly clear that Zorn's improvised body wrapping was not a convincingly regular human outfit. This incident, however unfortunate, initiated a steep learning curve about the rules of human body wrapping. The seven hundred volumes covering the full set of human body wrapping codes can be purchased separately, but the brief overview provided below should suffice for basic survival during a limited time.

One important variable to consider when choosing your human body wrapping is in which millennium – or even which century – your infiltration mission begins. This insight was first brought to us during infiltrator Zorn's early mission to Earth after his well-deserved twenty millennia-long holiday on the beaches of the oceanic world of Hoola-Loola. The fine sabre-tooth tiger fleece, which Zorn had taken the trouble of manually removing from a tiger before having a chance to learn just how much easier tigers are to defleece once they are dead, proved very useful for blending in among local human tribesmen of the Stone Age. The same fleece, although hardly worn and perfectly preserved (the vacuum capsule wardrobes at Hoola-Loolan hotels are top of the line) wasn't nearly as helpful in his efforts to blend in among the early renaissance French aristocracy inhabiting the same area several millennia later. Neither did the wrapping removed from an early renaissance French aristocrat help Zorn much in blending in among the inhabitants of the same Parisian suburb twenty generations later.

Because of the distorting effect time seems to have

on the human perception of wrapping, one and the same pair of trousers may thus evolve from incredibly attractive to appallingly shameful in the eyes of one and the same human during the course of that human's own lifetime. This conclusion has been supported by several experiments (including one in which the same pair of trousers was *not* actually worn for a whole lifetime before being presented to the subject for a second assessment).

Another important variable to consider is the cost of wrapping. Humans seem to believe that the greater financial damage a piece of apparel has inflicted on a human who wears it, the better it is. In effect, humans whose material well-being has suffered the most from acquiring their body wrapping are generally considered the best dressed. Of course, in reality, all human apparel looks equally ugly and there is little chance of assessing the amount of financial destruction any given rag has caused its human by simply looking at it. This could easily be remedied by having price tags attached to one's wrapping. Moreover, all human clothes have such tags to begin with. However, for some self-destructive reason humans insist on cutting these tags off before anyone else has had a chance to see them. Instead, they manifest the financial sacrifice they have made by means of cryptic signs, symbols and letter combinations embedded into the rags they wear. The variety of these signs is so great that few humans would recognise even a fraction of them, but the ones that are most recognised are usually seen on wrappings that inflict the greatest financial pain. We are not sure why wearing items with these signs evokes such respect and envy among other humans, but most likely it is a form of martyrdom – and humans are known to admire martyrs.

Using the above factors to determine which humans should be looked down upon or admired is a malicious phenomenon humans call "fashion". Combined with the pan-human compulsive wrapping disorder, fashion is one of the primary forces fuelling humanity's certain progression towards the destruction of their planet. It is truly a blessing to our ambitions of vacating Earth from humans before the end of the next century. Remember this when suffering through your daily dressing sessions and weekly shopping excursions. It should give you strength.

~

Collective Fuelling

As we have already established, humans are both fuelled by and produce organic matter. By tradition, they prefer sharing the fuelling process with other humans, but strangely seldom the production. An invitation to insert various forms of organic matter into one's mouth, grind them down with one's teeth, mix them with saliva and push them down one's oesophagus while using that same mouth to produce sonic communication signals in the company of other humans, is considered a friendly gesture. This tradition is so well-established that many humans use fuelling as a mere excuse to meet with other humans. An invitation to spend an evening producing humanium together is usually less well-received. Overall, although the production of humanium appears to be the only observable purpose of human existence, for some reason humans are tremendously ashamed of this process and always act as if they have absolutely nothing to do with it.

The variety of things humans may use as fuel for their body's operation is close to infinite. They have not yet learned to safely digest radioactive waste, but apart from that, there really is little left on this planet that humans haven't tried to consume. With that said, they tend to be very particular about how their fuel should be presented in order to be consumable, and what it should be accompanied with. Depending on this, one very same element may range from highly desirable to repulsively nauseating.

For instance, humans generally resent the idea of eating another living animal. However, cutting the animal up in pieces and holding it over fire for a brief period seems to completely alter that attitude. They gladly consume both freshly cut off pieces of fish bodies and frozen sweetened protein processed through a cow's body and chemically dyed during the same fuelling session, but they might kill you if you try to feed it all to them at the same time. In the rare cases when humans find something too appalling to consume, they mince it down into a sausage, put it into a sliced up pad made of grinded plant seeds mixed with whipped avian embryos, pour some red slime made out of squashed red plant seed capsules onto it and call it a hot dog (even though the share of minced dog in it is often negligible).

Timing is incredibly important to the way humans fuel up. They appear to uphold a sacred belief that fuel must be consumed at certain times of day in certain constellations they actually have names for. Nothing compromises an undercover alien better than a rib-eye steak for breakfast.

$\sim$

Etiquette

Many of the impractical and purposeless expectations humans have on each other go under the umbrella term "etiquette". Among these is the expectation that you should use the extremity of a limb that grows on one a particular side of your body for holding a particular fuel fragmentation tool during collective fuelling. They will expect it even if the said extremity is less skilled in holding tools than that of the equivalent limb growing on the other side of your body – or if it is presently engaged in a more important activity than separating fuel into tiny bits only to send them in the same direction as the rest of it.

The tool you must use for fuel fragmentation must

be picked from a very limited and rather clumsy toolset every human is always provided with when sharing the fuel with others. Using other tools is considered a breach of etiquette, so don't bother bringing your molecular splitter or magnetic lasso to human dinner parties. Even human-made tools other than those provided with the fuel are strongly advised against, as was reported by infiltrator Zorn, who once brought a saw to a steak dinner and registered the human host's predisposition rapidly deteriorating during the sawing.

Another element of etiquette is the mandatory utterance of certain phrases when certain specific events occur. One set of phrases must be uttered when a human you have encountered before becomes visible to you and is within audible proximity. Such phrases are known as "greetings" and have generally very little in common with each other apart from being compulsory to utter in this context. A greeting can be an adjective indicating a significant level of elevation. It can also be a positive assessment of the quality of the current time of day. (Accurate assessments do not qualify as greetings.) Greetings are usually accompanied by touching the emerging human's body. Which body part you touch, with which limb and with which intensity usually determines how well the greeting is received.

Another set of phrases is expected to be used when a human is about to become invisible to you and leave your range of audibility – be it by means of transportation or by drowning. At this point it is important to either tell the human that you see them, praise them for having made a good purchase or offer them a good day which you are not expected to deliver. We aren't sure why humans are so determined to pronounce these phrases every time, but most likely it is to ensure that the departing human does not change their mind about leaving.

As none of the aforementioned phrases provide any logical clues to their purpose, they are dangerously easy to mix up. Using a departure phrase as a greeting may be interpreted as a sign of hostility. If you are uncertain which one is which, simply wave the extreme part of your frontal appendage sideways.

One very specific phrase is expected to be uttered when another human, usually unintentionally, bursts a fountain of air and body liquid particles out into the atmosphere. The phrase suggests that the human should be rewarded for this outburst with a sacred deity's favour and protection. The phrase is only applicable when the aforementioned fountain (also known as a "sneeze") is erupted through the mouth.

～

Nocturnal Habits

Although humans generally feel a lot safer during daytime, for some reason they prefer to be in their most vulnerable state at night. In a previous chapter we have covered the concept of sleeping, which is the state in which humans are most susceptive to abduction. Do not be alarmed by their occasional roaring. As long as the human's eyes are closed and they aren't running – they are most probably hibernating.

To our great advantage, humans prefer to hibernate while lying down horizontally on top of elevated beds under their sacks of avian integument, with just enough space underneath them to position and calibrate your probing device. They also tend to remove all their body wrapping before hibernating, and place their only sheet of cover on top of themselves, leaving their primary points of entry exposed to assault from below. A minor inconvenience is that such easily accessible compartments underneath human beds appear to be very attractive to monsters, the presence of which may complicate your research.

Humans call their hibernation "sleeping", although they can be rather unpredictable in what they mean by it. Like most mammals, humans prefer sleeping next to other humans. However, when someone tells you that a human is sleeping with someone, you should not immediately assume it to be a good time to sneak into their bedroom with your research equipment. In fact, infiltrator Zorn's chronicles only mention one case when such an entry had been successful. According to the report, the humans who were said to be sleeping together were by no means asleep and appeared to have been warming up to Zorn's probing long before he arrived. Our counterintelligence first suspected a leak, but the subsequent persistence of Zorn's subjects in reciprocating his scientific efforts by means of devices much similar to his suggests that a much more sophisticated espionage scheme may have been at play.

∽

Keeping Clean

For a species inhabiting a planet which mostly consists of dirt, humans are remarkably uninclined to have any around them. Having as little dirt as possible on themselves and in their habitat is what humans call "keeping clean". Up until the last century or two, the most common way for humans to keep clean was to submerge themselves into the large silos of water mixed with organic waste and decomposed fish they call "seas" or "lakes" and rub away any visible dirt from their bodies, so that it would enrich the liquid composition of the silo, making it more welcoming to any other dirt that may be rubbed off into it from other human bodies.

In recent years this practice has become more recreational than hygienic, while keeping clean is something humans tend to do in places where the privacy of any removed dirt can be properly respected. Humans are particularly concerned about the cleanliness of their foremost appendages, which they wash thoroughly and often even when no dirt is visible on them. In order to preserve the flourishing bacterial microfauna they so eagerly cultivate on their hands by frequently pollinating door handles and elevator buttons, humans temporarily station any bacteria and other microorganisms inhabiting their palms on the surface of their hand-held gadgets between the washes.

~

The Concept of Winning

While the happiness of most intelligent species is primarily determined by each individual's general level of comfort, the happiness of humans is mostly determined by their perceived dominance over others. Applying basic logic to this principle would mean that only the most powerful human of all eight billion of them should be truly happy.

Fortunately for humans, this species is no strong ally of basic logic.

The dominance it requires to be happy doesn't necessarily need to be asserted in anything important, like cultural influence or the pace of technological progress. If you ever need to inflict great pride and joy upon a human – all you need to do is frame any random activity as a challenge and make sure that at least one other human performs it slightly less successfully.

Better yet, it does not even have to be performed by the human in question.

A human can experience profound happiness if anyone with whom the human in question believes to have any kind of association manages to assert dominance over someone else with whom this human does not wish to be associated, in just about any imaginable type of undertaking – no matter how pointless or insignificant.

Infiltrator Zorn once managed to get a human completely overwhelmed with joy just by ensuring that a certain mountain goat devoured a bowl of hot onion soup an instant faster than another mountain goat. An important prerequisite to the human's joy was the fact that the faster soup-eating goat originated from a hill next to a bush where the aforementioned human used to hide during his youth while spying on a neighbour's daughter showering. The human had no prior relationship with the goat that was an instant slower. This goat did, however, have a prior association with another human, who had previously made a claim that his associate goat was the fastest onion soup eater among mountain goats. This idea having been proven wrong was enough to assert one human's dominance over another in a specific area of competence. It is a notion humans call "winning".

Winning is so immensely important to humans that they are capable of extracting great pleasure from it even in contexts far less significant than mountain goats challenging each other in hot onion soup eating velocity. For instance, humans may experience a similar surge of joy when someone born in the same area of the planet's surface as them succeeds in placing a spherical airbag within a large rectangular frame against the wishes of those who strongly oppose such a placement while hypocritically attempting a similar placement in another frame against the wishes of others. These kinds of human activity are called "sports" and are the third greatest source of animosity between humans after religion and queue jumping.

It may be hard to comprehend why someone should care about who came in first or last in a run that isn't an escape from a vicious and deadly predator. It may not seem to make any difference who put a certain object where in a field – unless it is a minefield and the object is a mine. But do beware that complete indifference to sports would be seen as a very alien trait by most humans, so you would fare best by pretending to care.

Here is how you should do It. First, pick a sport. It should be a sport most humans would care about. There are hundreds of known human sports, but picking one that does not involve a ball would be perceived as almost as alien as not picking one at all. Second, pick a team to root for. "Rooting" means declaring your emotional loyalty to a group of humans wearing T-shirts of similar design whom you do not necessarily have any connection with and who will not in any way reward you for supporting them.

Once you have picked a team, you automatically declare all other teams and their supporters your personal rivals and use every opportunity to talk them down. Unless you like to be talked down yourself, make sure to pick a team that has at least some supporters among any humans you will have to interact with at some point. All the others will potentially want to harm you and may have to be eliminated at one point or another. Pretend to be overly excited whenever the team you have picked succeeds in doing something they get paid to do. Doing that in front of humans who support other teams will make you appear more authentically human, even though it may occasionally cost your human body some teeth.

Some sports are not really about winning. The human phenomenon of marathons proves that humans are able to extract gratification from virtually any achievement – even from running in a circle slightly faster than they did a year before. When someone shares an achievement like this with you – make your best attempt at looking impressed, however little sense it makes. Remember: humans are their own worst enemy, so if they wish to outrun themselves – who can blame them for trying?

~

Worship of the Natural

Although non-conformity with the natural ways of primate biology is what distinguishes humans from other apes, humans are obsessed with all things natural. Very few things humans do are natural to their species, but when a human tells you that something is natural, it is almost always meant as an endorsement.

For instance, humans much appreciate what they call "being close to nature". By that they usually mean spending time in one of the artificially developed agricultural areas easily distinguishable from the stratosphere as a yellow rectangle among many others scarring this poor planet's surface. Another human way of being close to nature is by surrounding themselves with trees. We are not sure why that is, but most probably it inspires pleasant fantasies about all the furniture they can make. Humans are generally strongly dependent on trees producing oxygen they need for breathing, but their general behavioural patterns suggest that they consider access to new furniture a lot more critical.

If a human tells you that the fuel they offer you is composed of natural ingredients, it usually means that it was unaffected by human technology and is therefore safe to consume. Humans have been developing various food processing technologies for many centuries, but none of these seem to have yet advanced beyond the point where not applying them at all would not be considered an advantage. Evidence shows that most humans would rather consume substances that have been processed through the digestive system of a cow and then infested by various forms of bacteria than similar looking and tasting substances synthesised in disinfected laboratory conditions by means of human technology.

Humans often use the adjective "natural" as an excuse for behaviours that disturb other humans. For instance, if you express your dissatisfaction with a human infant in the aeroplane seat next to you emitting various organic substances through all of its body openings and spreading them over a vast area, including your tray table and your hand luggage, its parent may remind you that such behaviour is natural, implicitly suggesting that it should be celebrated rather than frowned upon. As once proven through an experiment conducted by infiltrator Zorn, the same human might then express similar or even greater amounts of dissatisfaction if you perform a series of equivalently natural actions towards *them*.

"Unnatural", on the other hand, is an unflattering adjective, which humans often use when presented with new artificial ways of improving their hygiene, health or combating famine. It is also a common verbal attempt to correct mating behaviours that aren't intended for reproduction purposes. Such attempts usually have little immediate effect, but they do effectively inflict a profound burden of guilt, shame and misery upon the targeted humans, thereby indirectly shortening their average life expectancy and, as a consequence, decreasing the general occurrence of the deviant mating behaviour over time.

There are some exceptions to the general human glorification of all things natural which you should be aware of. One is following human instincts. You may occasionally hear humans encourage other humans to follow their instincts. We are not sure if they do it out of sheer malice or ignorance, but taking such advice can lead to disastrous consequences.

Human instincts are generally extremely counterproductive, which is why humans seldom follow them.

A contained experiment we once conducted, where a group of abducted humans were injected with a serum that disabled them from controlling their instincts, got out of hand so quickly that our experiment leader Zorn had to be evacuated from the lab before he could zip his trousers. The trousers had earlier been instinctively unzipped by a human subject who later had to be removed from Zorn by means of a highly complicated surgical intervention.

A human society where everyone follows their instincts wouldn't have been much worse than any other terrestrial animal society, had humans not been in the possession of weapons capable of annihilating their planet, which can be triggered by pressing a button designed and coloured to perfectly satisfy the human instinct of touching and pushing everything they shouldn't.

Another exception to the human preference of natural over artificial is the human body. Humans despise the most natural aspects of their body. They hate its smell and tend to suppress it by constantly rubbing themselves with artificial substances. They detest having hair in the vast majority of places on their body where it naturally grows, and when it begins to naturally disappear from places where they have the most of it, they resent that even more.

Most of all, humans abhor the energy reserves their bodies naturally build up during periods of excessive fuelling in order to secure survival during periods of fuel deficit. Even the smallest reserves ignite unproportionate amounts of anxiety, self-loathing and a firm determination to spend the reserved energy as soon as possible by exposing one's body to futile physical activity and imposing fuel rations. To understand this, you will need to familiarise yourself with the human concept of beauty.

∼

The Concept of Beauty

We have covered the importance of beauty to humans with regard to their bodies and how you can use it as a trick to win their predisposition by complimenting them. Such tricks do not actually require you to understand the human concept of beauty, but there are cases where this understanding can be vitally important, such as when you need to additionally boost a human's opinion of you by giving them a present.

Humans rarely appreciate gifts they find hideous, especially if the gift is an element of habitat I or a piece of body wrapping. There is no certain way of knowing what a human would consider beautiful and not. However, there are some common denominators that are worth remembering.

One common denominator is symmetry. There is a reason why almost all human buildings are so unimaginatively rectangular and why humans with very asymmetrical bodies usually struggle with finding a mate. The human brain is so slow and primitive that any observed geometrical variation consumes a great share of its computing power, resulting in fatigue and frustration. You may occasionally observe such frustration manifesting itself in humans jumping angrily on their suitcases, which they have packed with an excessive number of unevenly shaped apparel items in a manner that signals lacking awareness of the geometrical shape of the suitcase.

The same goes for any item. The more symmetrical it is, the less likely that humans would consider it ugly. If it is a cupboard, the drawers should be symmetrically placed. If it is a ground vehicle, the wheels should be symmetrically sized and shaped. If it is a pet animal, then its limbs, eyes and ears had better be symmetrical.

Most clearly the human obsession with symmetry manifests itself in human architecture. It is virtually impossible to find an asymmetric human made building that doesn't self-destruct shortly after being erected. Over ninety percent of all human-made buildings have a rectangular shape – the most primitive geometric shape that exists, but also a very symmetric one. The few things humans make that aren't symmetric they either call "defective" or "artistic".

Another common denominator in the human concept of beauty is remoteness from human influence. This applies particularly well to ambiances and background scenery. The less a landscape is affected by humans, the more beautiful humans tend to find it and the more likely they are to want to pose in front of it when taking pictures. Few things are more satisfying to a human than looking at a vast landscape where no humans are present. (To be fair, this is a sentiment they share with the vast majority of the animal kingdom.) Strangely, this doesn't seem to have any observable influence on the human propensity to be present just about everywhere – and to keep modifying the planet' surface in a way that makes human presence most apparent.

Some human beauty standards you will find shocking beyond comprehension. For instance, humans are eerily fascinated by the reproductive organs of plants. This fascination sometimes takes on bizarre forms where plant genitals are cut off, assembled in symmetrical arrangements and presented to other humans as much appreciated gifts to be placed in a moist vessel and marvelled at while they slowly die. Some humans like to be depicted next to such arrangements of amputated plant genitals, misguidedly believing that this will make them appear more attractive in the photo (in most cases it rather makes the plant genitals appear more attractive).

This morbid fascination with plant genitalia is so deeply entrenched in human culture that there are, in fact, plant breeding camps where millions of plants are deliberately conceived and nurtured on an industrial scale every year, only to have their genitals cut off and sold to wholesalers across the planet. The ultrasonic screams of terror and torment from mutilated terrestrial plants can be heard all the way to the populated worlds of Saturn's asteroid belt and are just one of many reasons why Earth still is a no-go zone for the galactic plant tourism industry.

∾

An Eye for an Eye

An ancient human code of justice known as "An eye for an eye" suggests that any amount of suffering caused by a human should be compensated with an equivalent amount of suffering bestowed upon that same human, thereby correcting the perceived imbalance of experienced discomfort. Although this code has been officially discontinued in most human societies, most humans still appear to extract immense amounts of satisfaction from enacting such corrections. Humans refer to such corrective action as "revenge" and find it extremely gratifying, despite the obvious lack of any perceivable benefit.

Aiding a human in enacting revenge upon their wrongdoer can be an easy way of winning the human's affection. Be warned, however, that the symmetry of retribution suggested by the term "an eye for an eye" is not always perfectly generalisable. A human who has lost an eye due to another human's malicious actions may indeed deeply appreciate you bringing them the eye of the perpetrator. A human who was murdered may not equally appreciate you murdering their killer, as dead humans are known to be generally insensitive and ungrateful. Stealing from a thief may also generate varying results. You should definitely not seek to aid humans in symmetrically avenging sexual assault. All these insights were brought to our knowledge by our pioneer infiltrator Zorn, whose multiple attempts to win favour with molested humans by offering them the opportunity to molest their molesters as retribution were largely unsuccessful.

~

INTERACTING WITH IMAGINARY OBJECTS

When you see a human intensively scratching their crotch with their right hand while holding up and squeezing an invisible sponge with their left, take notice of the surrounding sonic ambience. If you find it saturated with loud distorted noise, then what you are observing is most likely what humans call "playing air guitar". It is one of the least explored human behaviours, but one that is very much expected to be exhibited when you are exposed to the aforementioned noise. If you aren't proficient enough in operating your human body to be able to coordinate the movement of your limbs in such a manner, the second best option would be to nod your head violently to the noise.

Air guitar is just one of multiple human codes of interacting with invisible objects. Some of these interactions are expected to be exhibited when hearing certain sounds. If you find yourself among a large group of angry humans who suddenly begin chanting the same phrase in unison over and over, you may need to pretend to punch at an imaginary object above your head every time the phrase is uttered. If you notice that humans aren't heeding your warnings, you may want to accompany your next warning by pointing your finger at that same imaginary object. If you master this skill well, you may even make some extra money by charging humans for speaking with their imaginary dead relatives.

~

GLORIFICATION OF DEATH

Like most terrestrial organisms, humans are mortal. It means that the final goal in their life is to become completely immobile and slowly decompose into a fertiliser of mediocre quality. Reaching this goal is called "being dead" and is a state that appears to evoke immense respect and admiration among other humans. Evidence shows that even the most unpopular humans are indulged with praise and veneration as a result of simply dying. Amateur alien infiltrators are often tempted to take advantage of this odd ethic to gain some easily earned social points with humans, but please only use this as a last resort, as dying gravely complicates further undercover work.

Humans have a peculiar habit of placing dead humans in wooden vessels and storing them in carefully arranged underground compartments labelled with names and dates. The exact purpose of such meticulousness is still a mystery to science, but its obvious similarity to aged wine production certainly provides a clue. Going through all this trouble with boxing and labelling only makes sense if the stored objects are meant to be extracted at a later stage. Such extraction does indeed happen. Humans call it "archaeology". It involves having the remains of the human bodies dusted, examined and moved to new, equally organised and labelled compartments, presumably for further ageing.

You can get access to a lot of valuable research material without ever having to abduct a human just by pretending to be an archaeologist. The only downside is that you need to wait for at least a hundred years between burying and extracting the human. Infiltrator Zorn has repeatedly reported that humans can get very sentimental when dead humans they know are unearthed before they are sufficiently aged and decomposed.

Due to the above, if you pretend to die only to gain some favour with humans, you will either have to lie still underground for a century or two before going back to your infiltration business, which would be a poor investment of your time to say the least, or you will have to sneak out early. The latter is better done at night, when fewer humans can be expected to entertain themselves by visiting burial grounds. It would be your best chance of getting out unnoticed and sparing yourself the scolding for not being properly aged, not to mention the possible long-term effects on the general human worldview.

Humans are quite hypocritical in their attitude towards death. While deeply mourning the deaths of other humans, they really prefer them to stay dead. Judging by their cinematography, the mere idea of dead humans coming back to life appears to be their greatest nightmare. It is unclear where this specific fear comes from, but infiltrator Zorn's multiple graveyard escapades after trying to score some cheap social points with humans may have had something to do with it.

There are ways you can harness this strange human fascination with death to win favour with them without actually having to die or pretending to be dead. One of the side effects of this bizarre death cult is that even being close to death can win you human admiration. In other words, if you constantly try to die by exposing yourself to lethal danger, humans will respect and admire you almost as much as if you were truly dead. A habit of doing so, and thereby dramatically decreasing one's life expectancy, is a self-preservation instinct malfunction called "courage" and is a highly praised trait in many human societies. Typical courageous behaviours you may consider are jumping over deep crevices, expressing unpopular opinions publicly or talking in a disrespectful tone to someone whose hands are engaged in a firm grip around the shaft of a large axe.

～

FIDELITY

During your infiltration mission you may need to assume marital status with another human for the sake of conspiracy. Doing so will require a thorough understanding of one of the most irrational and contradictory human codes – the code of fidelity. In essence, it means that once two humans have engaged in a coupling ritual, they are obliged to declare a feud against nature and suppress their basic procreation instincts by denying themselves the pleasure of coupling with other humans and thus severely arresting the spread of their DNA. Violating this code is one of the most certain ways of getting in trouble with humans and is, by sheer coincidence, also the primary cause of most inter-human conflicts.

This may seem an easy enough rule to follow at a glance, but many infiltrators fall victim to unintentional misinterpretations of this code, which has already caused more world wars than humanity can remember due to its occasional annihilation. The main reason for these misinterpretations is, as it often is with humans, the vagueness of definitions.

Humans still aren't in full agreement on what really defines coupling. Their fidelity expectations towards other humans are therefore seldom fully aligned. Different humans may develop fidelity expectations on different grounds. The easiest ones are those who require the vows of fidelity to be clearly expressed in front of an assembly of witnesses. It is beyond this point that you will need to undertake additional secrecy measures when performing your abductions.

There are, however, those who will expect you to enact the code of fidelity after simply spending a fair amount of time in their company and touching certain parts of their body. Infiltrator Zorn has had to be evacuated from Earth more than once after being chased by mobs of outraged former abduction subjects, who had completely misinterpreted the scientific purpose of the instrumental body examinations he had subjected them to.

Despite the aforementioned vagueness of definitions, most humans agree that touching the body of a human who is not one's assigned partner is a transgression against the code of fidelity. As perfect adherence to this rule would have made human life extremely impractical, humans have come to agree on certain safe zones on their body that should be completely or partially exempt from this rule. To our knowledge, these is no document specifying exactly which these zones are, but Zorn's tireless experiments with groping and grabbing around have allowed us to deduct – by method of exclusion – that the only human body parts which are perfectly safe to touch at any point without invoking infidelity claims are the upper arms and the ugly knob at the front of the human head known as "the nose".

It is common for drowning and otherwise distressed humans to reach out their hands to whoever is standing by, but you should always resist the impulse of grabbing them. Holding another human's hand is perceived as very intimate and therefore easily deemed as an act of infidelity. You should also be mindful that pulling at the upper arm of a human who is being sucked down into a pit of quicksand carries a high risk of your hand gradually sliding towards theirs. To avoid this trap, we recommend that you always go for the only safe option which – also by method of exclusion – is the nose. The grip you may get around most human noses will usually be far from perfect, but the worst thing that can happen if your hand slides is that you will lose your grip and the human drowns. Your fidelity to your assigned human partner will remain unquestioned.

The mechanism by which the code of fidelity is enforced is known as jealousy. Jealousy is a human method of sustaining inner misery by effectively converting a given amount of happiness observed in others into an equal amount of self-torture. Essentially, jealousy is a perverted form of another human code known as "envy", which is a common human response to any other human enjoying anything that the prior human isn't enjoying. When the amount of pain the envious human inflicts on themselves becomes unbearable, they tend to inflict pain upon others. For this reason you are advised to avoid making humans envious. The safest way of doing so is to never enjoy anything in front of anyone. Only be happy when on your own, use every social interaction as an opportunity to demonstrate just how miserable you are – and you will never have to suffer an envious human.

～

Lying and Joking

Lying is a human concept of saying things that contradict reality. Its purpose is to adjust the liar's audience's perception of reality to best fit the liar's interests. Lying is so deeply embedded in human culture that it is absolutely impossible to get anywhere on Earth without lying.

From the moment of your first contact with humans you will become the target of multiple kinds of questions, in response to which you will need to lie in order to maintain your human cover. Expect questions like "How are you?", "Where are you from?", "Did you have a nice weekend?", "Do I look fat?", "Do you think I'm some kind of animal?", "Are you carrying any weapons or explosives?" or "Do you swear to tell the truth, the whole truth and nothing but the truth?" and always lie in response. An honest response to any of these will get you in trouble, one way or another.

It is easy to be tricked into believing that, only because humans lie all the time, they should equally appreciate being lied to. They don't. In fact, bragging to humans about what a great lie you just told them may severely complicate your covert operations. Lies are really only useful for as long as humans believe them to be the truth. Inexperienced infiltrators often overdo their lying efforts by constantly saying things that contradict observable reality. If you ever find yourself describing something a human is presently looking at as the opposite of what it is, try to save your credibility by pretending to be ironic.

Irony is a type of lie, the purpose of which is to make the truth even more evident. However, be warned that irony is only discernible when making judgemental or subjective statements. It may work if you make a remark like "This aardvark is very attractive" when in fact the mammal in question appears to be undeniably off-putting. It will, however, not work if you make a factual statement that is evidently false, like "This grizzly bear is exclusively herbivore" when referring to a mammal in the process of devouring the human you are speaking to.

In cases like this, your second fall-back option would be to pretend that you are joking. As was explained in a previous chapter, jokes are lies that are so unequivocally remote from truth that their bare utterance inflicts temporary human brain malfunction leading to uncontrollable outbursts of laughter. If you hear the human in the process of being devoured by the grizzly bear laugh, then you know you have succeeded.

The biggest human lie of all is their desire for truth. Humans are completely incapable of handling truth and they only really appreciate honesty when it makes them feel good, which it seldom does. These overgrown bonobos are so scared of the truth that they may even get offended by it. Whenever a human asks you to be honest – be sure that what they are really asking you to do is tell them what they want to hear.

Anything else you may say they will most likely use against you.

~

Recycling Names

There are over eight billion humans on Earth alone (the number of the abducted ones held in various labs and zoological farms across the galaxy is not exactly known). Naturally, each human is given an individual name at birth. One could argue that telling humans apart strictly by appearance is hard enough, so you would at least expect the names to be of some help. Yet, humans do not use names to simplify identification and promote individuality. On the contrary, the human naming tradition seems to put privacy protection above all.

Not only do humans name their offspring with names that already exist. The most common human way of deciding a child's name is by picking one of the currently most popular names in their planetary area, thereby minimising the child's risk of being identified as a separate individual. An almost equally common (and almost equally shrewd) method of naming a human child is by using the name of a close relative, thereby also minimising identification risks during collective fuelling sessions together with humans of the same genome branch.

~

Keeping Busy

Humans frequently refer to themselves as "human beings", which may leave you with the false impression that simply being is something they frequently do. Nothing could be further from the truth. Humans are obsessed with keeping themselves busy at all times.

If you ask a human what they are doing and the response is "Nothing", you can be quite sure that the human is lying to cover up some malicious scheme. Whenever a human finishes a task and has no other apparent task to switch to, they immediately begin searching for one.

Humans find doing nothing to be such an extraordinary activity, that they even have a word for it. They call it "meditation" and it takes an average human some extensive learning and practice to master this art of not doing anything for more than five seconds. Most humans never really master it.

Having said this, please mind the distinction between "doing nothing" and "doing nothing useful". The prior is the most inhuman thing there is, while the latter, on the contrary, is the primary feature of the human modus operandi.

This is something you will need to consider when infiltrating. You should never behave or look as if you aren't busy doing something. If a human notices you simply standing and staring, it will raise their suspicions about whether or not you are indeed human –

especially if you are staring straight at them, and especially if you are doing it at night.

If you cannot think of anything you absolutely have to do at a given moment (which will be the case most of the time), you should at least pretend that you are doing something. The easiest way to do so is to hold up a human made mobile device with your hands and drum at its screen with your thumbs at uneven intervals, while staring intensely at it. This trick is also a convenient method of avoiding engaging in a conversation with a human who has chosen you as a remedy for their lack of means to keep themselves busy.

For most humans, such means are usually quite superfluous. An average human typically spends most of their day either depleting planetary resources or producing means by which to deplete them. For this, the human is rewarded with other such means, which they effectively use to procure products of planetary resource depletion. Any time that is left over between these activities humans tend to invest in making and raising more humans in order to multiply the speed of planetary resource depletion.

In the unlikely event of any additional time becoming available, humans immediately fill it with a special type of entirely purposeless activities they call "hobbies". Human hobbies include a variety of activities ranging from moving oneself between different distant points on the planet's surface, catching and killing other living organisms, modifying the composition and appearance of various useless items – to producing strange sounds, combating other humans, making two-dimensional depictions of the surrounding (and perfectly observable) environment, collecting large quantities of useless items of a specific type or pretending to be someone else and behaving in an exactly predetermined order together with other humans doing the same.

It is highly advisable that you choose any such hobby for yourself and engage in it every time you happen to not be busy doing something else. Should you ever find yourself in a situation where no activity is possible to perform – pretend to hibernate. Hibernation is essentially the only state in which being idle is socially acceptable if you are a human. Just make sure not to do it for too long, or else humans may mistakenly cremate you.

$\sim$

Zorn search party telepathic intercom transmission excerpt 5

Transmitted 4 hours and 54 minutes after dispatch. The human speech has been converted into readable telepathic signals for better understanding.

Balbooza: [*Gee, I have a bad feeling about that human approaching us really fast.*]
Gee: [*Is it because of our unfortunate encounter with*

those bald homos earlier? It was just poor timing, you know. And you have to admit that I was right about you looking perfectly human. None of them looked the least surprised when they tore off your head scarf.]

Balbooza: [*It's not that. The fur on this one's head looks like he has just suffered an immense electric shock, the pins and spikes on the black-dyed animal skin he is wearing do not seem to have any conceivable purpose other than to inflict pain, he has a dense aura of bacterial fauna around him, is clearly intoxicated with a personality-altering substance and his movement trajectory suggests a confrontation probability of eighty-seven point—*]

Human: You! You're that monkey that stole my trousers! Give them back right now, you little shit!

Gee: [*This is interesting. Balbooza, I am sure you know this already, but chimpanzees cannot talk. Please do not blow our cover, and leave the talking to me.*]

Human: Is this your monkey? It stole my—

Gee: Mooghh mghh mguugh—

Balbooza: [*Gee, perhaps you should remove that diving nozzle from your mouth when speaking.*]

Gee: [*Good idea.*] Mister human man, if indeed you are a man [*Remember, Balbooza, one should never assume a human's gender based on their appearance.*], I am afraid you are mistaken. This here is no other than another ordinary human man. His name is... Humanoid Manson. He is a janitor. He also suffers from a speech impediment and has kindly asked me to administer all sonic communication with other humans on his behalf.

Human: Wow, missy, that's one sexy outfit you got there... Please, don't cover yourself up for my sake, **unintelligible throat sounds**!

Gee: Oh, this... Just a small incident involving shaving a primate – who is not currently present – with a walrus tusk.

Human: Well, this mister Manson of yours is wearing my trousers and I want them back. Right now!

Gee: Mister human man, are you positively sure that these are your trousers?

Human: Yes, miss human woman, I'm positively fucking sure. The bastard stole them yesterday night. Totally ruined my evening, I tell ya.

Gee: Could you please tell me what happened?

Human: Well, I'd say that's a bit... private. But hey, you don't look like you care much about privacy, so what the heck... Me and my lads, we were camping out here at the festival. Had a few cold ones with some sweet lasses from that tent right over there. Found myself having a bit of a good time with one pretty miss. Then all of a sudden I see this little prick sneaking away with my trousers, so I call him out. "Hey, you dirty monkey!" I say. "Get back here with my trousers before I come over and smack up your hairy monkey arse!" The second time I say the word "monkey" he stops, looks down at himself, then looks back at me and then at my gal. That's when it all goes bonkers, 'cause the girl, she starts twitching and shit. Must be epilipstic or something. Then she pulls on her top, turns around and takes off. Never saw her again. And this little bugger, he took off too – with my trousers! The whole thing ruined! Now why the hell would you train a monkey to behave like that?

Gee: [*Balbooza, are you copying this?*]

Balbooza: [*Sorry, I was just looking up the word "epilipstic". Did the human say anything substantial?*]

Gee: [*Very much so. I think we are one step closer to finding Zorn.*] Mister human man, I understand your concern and am willing to remedy the situation by helping you retrieve your desired object of unsolicited public fornication. What was that human female's name?

Human: How the hell should I know? She had big tits – that did it for me, **unintelligible throat sounds**.

Gee: Well, then what did she look like, apart from having generous mammary glands?

Human: Fake blonde, short green top, had a Mickey Mouse tattoo on her right thigh... Did I say she had big tits?

Gee: You did. Thank you, this should be enough for us to find Zo... Find *her*.

Human: Yeah, cool. Now, how about giving me those trousers back?

Balbooza: [*Gee, we cannot give him the trousers. Everyone will see that I am a chimpanzee if I don't wear trousers.*]

Gee: I'm afraid I cannot do that. But you may have my trousers instead.

Human: Well, that sounds like a horseshit's worth of a deal, considering that you're wearing a diving suit.

But... I gotta say, I might consider it just to see you take it off, **unintelligible throat sounds**.

Gee: Well, it's settled then.

Balbooza: [*Gee, while you are removing your last pieces of human clothing in full public sight, could you please explain to me why you are so interested in that human female who successfully evaded intercourse with this repulsive creature you just spoke to?*]

Gee: [*Because she is Zorn. Don't you get it? When the human called him a "monkey" twice, Zorn must have realised his body wasn't human and decided to quickly jump bodies while he still had some body infiltration energy surge left. Of the closest two human host bodies he obviously chose the least ugly one. Now, let us figure out what a Mickey Mouse tattoo is.*]

Balbooza: [*I just scanned the human's mind. I did not enjoy it. A tattoo is a kind of voluntary artificial corruption of a human's skin with an ink image that blurs out with age. Mickey Mouse is a mythical creature created by a human named Walter Disney. It looks like a mix between a rodent under severe substance influence and an extremely undernourished human with abnormally swollen extremities.*]

Gee: [*Sounds disgusting.*]

Balbooza: [*It is.*]

Gee: [*Well, let's think. Zorn is an experienced infiltrator. He knows that the best way of keeping a low profile among humans is to behave as they would in his place. He also knows that if someone looking for him figured out which human host he is using, they would try to find* *that host human where it is most likely to be. Where might someone with that kind of marking live?*]

Balbooza: [*I don't know, but during my scan of the human's brain there was one place where both Mickey Mouse and Walter Disney appeared a lot. It is called Disneyland.*]

Gee: [*Then that is where we are going next. There is just one thing that is bothering me...*]

Balbooza: [*Is it that oxygen tank you keep carrying on your back? The straps must be tough on your skin now that you are no longer wearing that rubber suit.*]

Gee: [*No, it's just that I cannot make any sense of why Zorn would try to steal this human's trousers...*]

Balbooza: [*Well, while scanning the human's brain I learned that not wearing any clothes in public is a major human taboo. Zorn may have known that.*]

Gee: [*Oh.*] Mister human man, may I please ask you to divert your attention away from studying my human body for a moment? I need you to give me all of your clothes.

Chapter 6

Human Belief Systems

To most sentient creatures in the galaxy, knowledge is one-dimensional: there are things you know and things you don't know. Somehow, humans have managed to add a second dimension to knowledge which they call "belief". Simply put, belief means acting as if you know things you cannot possibly know. Such behaviour is typically caused by superstition. Superstition is a glitch in the human brain that can be conveniently used to compulsively provoke desired human behaviours by suggesting a causal relationship between any two random events.

This glitch was scientifically confirmed through a black cat experiment infiltrator Zorn ran some centuries ago. In the experiment, Zorn would let a black cat pass in front of a human subject, who was unknowingly headed towards an abduction zone. After a rather intensive examination the subject would be released – only to be abducted and examined again the next day right after another black cat had been passed in front of the subject. It would normally take three to four iterations before the subjects would conclude that black cats were omens of bad luck – a belief that quickly spread through word of mouth and which persists until this day. It is, in fact, the primary reason why many cats dye their fur black in order to avoid being petted. One exception is Britain, where the human subjected to the aforementioned experiment stoically presented his experience to other Brits as "very character-building and a splendid learning oppor-tunity", accidentally leading his countrymen into the superstitious belief that black cats are, in fact, an omen of *good* luck. Zorn's hypothesis was nevertheless proven in both cases.

A set of superstitions put together into a joint narra-tive is what humans call a "religion". Religion adds a lot of additional flavour to the already mostly irrational human behaviour. Its most easily observable purpose is to usher humans into behavioural patterns they would otherwise never have adopted – either because these patterns defy common sense or because they contradict basic human instincts.

For example, religion may compel humans to dress in a manner that dramatically decreases their chances of procreation. Even in times of prosperity and plenty, when humans have no immediate urgency to compete for resources, religion provides additional reasons for animosity, keeping humans busy with building defences and waging wars instead of exploring space and infesting other planets.

Even when no objective reasons for hate and resentment between humans are available, religion offers the means of providing them by imposing behavioural codes which are impossible to fully adhere to without feeling resentment against those who don't. On many occasions religion has inspired humans to actively decrease their current population in order to increase religious unity.

In all these respects, human religion is perfectly aligned with the interests of the universe and should therefore be nurtured and encouraged. Infiltrating human religious institutions not only provides many possibilities to exert broad influence over the human population, but also offers multiple convenient opportunities to perform various experimental research on human children without their parents protesting. To avoid being compromised when apprehended performing such research, you will need to familiarise yourself with some of the following religious concepts.

~

THE CONCEPT OF GOD

Most humans are paranoid. They believe that they are being constantly watched and controlled by an invisible being that will punish them for every wrong they commit. They sometimes talk to that being in its

absence, as if they had some sort of long-distance trans-
mitter in their heads, asking it to forgive them for the
wicked things they did to other humans and thanking it
for the fuel they have purchased themselves and are
about to consume.

Humans call this being "God". The term likely
originates from infiltrator Zorn's rather too honest
attempt to explain to a prehistoric human why a
terraforming vehicle from the Galactic Operations
Department (G.O.D.) was parked outside the human's
cave. Knowing that terrestrial mammals express
curiosity by sniffing and licking their objects of interest,
Zorn concluded that the caveman desired a thorough
explanation of how a terraformer works. Galvanised by
this primitive creature's admirable pursuit of knowledge, the great infiltrator did his best to explain how the
terraformer created Earth.

The explanation covered how the G.O.D. construction vehicle first needed to extinguish the lava by
covering the planet with a hydraulic foil, then dissolve
the planet's thick cloud cover by assembling all volcanic
dust from the atmosphere around an orbiting magnet
now known as the "Moon" in order to let the sunlight in
and then elevate parts of the underlying rock to create
dry land areas suitable for landing and finally inject
organic seeds to create the biosphere.

According to Zorn's report, the caveman proved to
be a grateful audience, only occasionally interrupting
the narrative by pounding his hairy chest with his
equally hairy fists (presumably in agreement).

However, when passing the explanation on to his tribe, the enlightened human resolved to reduce the story to a brief executive summary, with a couple of minor inaccuracies thrown in for dramatic purposes.

The summary stated that G.O.D. had created Earth and everything else around it (humans initially referred to the rest of the universe as "heaven"), and that Earth was initially a rather dull place until G.O.D. called in some light by means of some sophisticated voice assistant and was mightily pleased to see it. The summary also claimed that at the time when the planet was created, its rotation did not provide the necessary daylight variations and thus light needed to be manually separated from darkness, which is something G.O.D. was also unjustly credited for.

The description of G.O.D.'s terraforming procedure was further distorted as it spread through word of mouth during the course of the subsequent 20,000 years and spawned numerous different religions as a result. Most of them share the worldview where the universe is governed by a totalitarian supreme power that holds a monopoly on truth and constantly spies on everyone. It is accepted that all opposition to this deity is demonised in all public channels and its sympathisers are banned from influence and condemned to eternal torture. Although this part is remarkably accurate, the remaining backstory of nearly every human religion would likely strike you as uncompromisingly remote from any conceivable reality.

Nearly all human religions seem to firmly reject the

idea that humans owe their origins to a bonobo accidentally walking into an Australopithecus cave with a truss of fermented mangos. Instead, most of them insist on the notion that some deity deliberately created them in its own image. There is yet no evidence of a creature as hideous as a human and possessing the capability of creating new species ever having existed anywhere else in the universe. It is also highly unlikely that a creature that looks like a human would have the capability of single-handedly creating a world. However, as you will soon notice, the point of human belief is to act as if something that is supported by little or no evidence is unambiguously true.

Humans are a lot less religious today than ever before. The average number of gods humans believe in is currently in the range of zero to one per capita. The gods have become more similar too, all sharing the common trait of supposedly being able to see and know everything every human does, thinks and wants. All the four major human gods – Allah, Jehovah, Meta and Google – would appear to be equally proficient in it. Human religions founded around more than one god are scarce and some even actively impose a one god policy (presumably in order to avoid divine inflation of the kind that can be observed on the theocratic world of Prayonis, with its average forty-seven gods per capita and an average divinity level per god so low that most gods are completely socially marginalised and confined to urban slums).

One of the major human religions has outdone the

others and managed to bring its god count to zero. This religion is called Buddhism and is the one most praised and encouraged by extraterrestrials, as its main purpose is essentially for its followers to stop being human and perish from existence by just sitting and doing nothing long enough.

Unfortunately, the vast majority of humans follow less constructive religions which strongly encourage humans to keep procreating. Regrettably, this also applies to the largest two. In this guide we will be concentrating only on one of these (the one whose followers have of late been exhibiting the lowest average propensity of murdering you for inaccurately describing it).

The religion we will focus on is called Christianity and is founded on the idea of one almighty, loving and forgiving god, who is both a father, a son and the ghost of a deceased pigeon. This may sound like a lot, but our research shows that quite many dead pigeons match the description of having been both a father and a son. This circumstance makes the notion of this god having created humans in its own image somewhat unlikely. Although humans bear a much larger resemblance to pigeons than to any extraterrestrial organism, the differences are significant enough for us to be able to describe this zoological self-portrait attempt as a failure.

The Christian god is believed to be a loving one. So loving, in fact, that he (humans seem convinced that their god is a male, despite appearing to be the only existing specimen of its species), is believed to love all humans. (This is the one part where they are being at least moderately consistent, as any creature would need to be nothing short of almighty to be able to love each and every one of these eight billion terrestrial parasites.)

If by now you have succeeded in understanding the concept of human love and learned to recognise its various manifestations, then you may find the apparent manifestations of the Christian god's love somewhat counterintuitive. It supposedly includes unleashing locust attacks, deadly plagues, infanticide and turning a blind eye to numerous occurrences of manslaughter, world wars and genocide.

According to what Christian humans view as sacred scriptures, their almighty and infinitely wise god is extremely sensitive to humans not behaving in accordance with his specific instructions. He is said to have punished the first two humans he ever made for consuming a certain product of terrestrial vegetation by sending them off to live a life of misery, spawn offspring and then have their offspring mate with each other in order to create more humans. Once this chain of incest had produced enough humans to no longer consider each other family, god is said to have started growing increasingly concerned about what he believed was irresponsible sexual behaviour and overall moral decay. To remedy that, the all-loving and merciful deity is believed to have flooded the planet with water, drowning not only all humans, but all land-living creatures except for one couple of each species, so that they could all go back to the morally righteous practice of procreating through incest again.

The latter is, of course, a distorted version of the N.O.A.H. (Naval Operation for Animal Harvest) project chronology. When G.O.D. had sanctioned the two million year long lease of Earth by Aquarius Industries Ltd. for the purpose of building the third largest planetary aquarium in the Milky Way, it was contingent on extracting a sample of various land-living terrestrial species to be bred in a less hazardous planetary environment uninfested by humans.

Agent Zorn, who was then a clerk at the department responsible for the extraction budget, thought it wise to employ a human subcontractor to construct the colony ship that would transport the terrestrial fauna sample to its destination. The subcontractor, a ragged farmer who had made a very convincing pitch of himself as a proficient shipbuilder, offered to build the ship at a great discount. This allowed the department to invest the saved budget surplus in a terrestrial mammal aphrodisiac production plant, for which a new and promising venture called Z.O.R.N. Enterprises Ltd. had coincidentally secured a construction lot right next to the breeding colony.

At the time, Zorn had spent very little time on Earth and had not been duly informed that humans are primitive carnivore apes whose most advanced means of travel at the time were carts made of dead vegetation propelled by extremely stubborn four-legged ungulates. As the construction progressed it became increasingly clear that the N.O.A.H. builder's idea of a ship was a lot less interstellar than Zorn had anticipated. The aquarium construction had to be aborted after it was discovered that the colony ship actually never left the planet and was idly floating on its aquatic surface, releasing such vast daily quantities of excrement into the sea that it posed a serious hazard to the marine life of the aquarium.

Mass genocide and bizarre consumption restrictions are quite common types of conduct for various human gods, but where the Christian faith really stands out is how its impeccably righteous god manages to impregnate a betrothed woman, who later gives birth to the most popular human in history, Jesus Christ. The latter managed to amass an unprecedentedly large social following, but was later cancelled and deplatformed for saying something that didn't fit into the socially acceptable narrative of the time.

There is some mention of god bestowing health and prosperity upon some humans, but such blessing seems to have been exclusively granted to true loyalists and very rarely to critics of god's value set and management style. Moreover, humans who believe in god are convinced that if they fail to adhere to their god's preferred code of conduct, their all-loving and merciful creator will send them to a place of such horrific torment that even our most dated and ill-equipped human research facilities would seem like a stroll in zero gravity by comparison. C-level church executives are usually exempt from this hazard, provided that they express regret about all the lives they have ruined no later than a millisecond before they become incapacitated to ruin any more for the reason of being dead.

Even for an extremely primitive and inherently manic species like humans, accepting these stories as an accurate description of reality would require a grave defect in critical thinking, which is why spreading such beliefs usually needs to be aided by large quantities of disproportionate violence. Fortunately for the cause, humans are remarkably talented in turning prophetic teachings about love and piety into causes for genocide. If even an all-loving god can deliberately cause a flood that kills off half of the planet's biosphere, then a human following his word certainly can obliterate a couple of million other non-believers just to prove a point.

≈

THE THEISM OF THEYISM

For a long time it was believed that humans were divided by religion, with each god having its own exclusive following that did not recognise the other gods. More careful studies of human religious behaviours later revealed that apart from all the various human gods, there is one universal god in whom absolutely all humans believe – regardless of their religious affiliation. The worship of this deity seems to be shrouded with secrecy. We have not been able to find any scriptures, temples or clerics, but the presence of this secret belief is noticeable in casual conversations among humans all over the planet.

The worshipped deity of this religion is so secretive that it never seems to be mentioned by name, but only by the pronoun "they", which is why we call this religion "Theyism". You will recognise its followers by their ambiguous mention of "them" in contexts where no obvious subject is present or easily identifiable.

"They" are the only known gender-neutral human god. They are considered truly almighty and expected to be able to correct every wrong in the world – big or small. "I hope They'll fix that sign soon." you may hear a human driver say when passing by a broken road sign or hear another exclaim "Wow, look! They've set up an ice cream shop right next to the beach." Unless there is a group of people with toolboxes standing right in front of the human when phrases like this are uttered, you can be reasonably sure the human is referring to the higher power of Theyism.

If you need to make a human believe anything you tell them, start with "They say…" and whatever comes after will become indisputable. A true Theyist will never ask for the source of your information. If They say so, then so it must be.

A rather unfortunate consequence of this belief is that many things in human society that need fixing are actually never fixed because so many humans who are perfectly capable of fixing them are so convinced that the almighty They will handle it. Many don't even bother researching other options but simply assume that They have it all under control.

Interestingly, unlike all other gods, who are usually only mentioned in reverence and fear, They are often the object of human criticism and scorn. You may hear a human say: "Why the hell did They pile up all this junk in front of our door?!" or "They might as well have placed that parkometer on the moon!" or "Don't They ever flush around here?" You will never hear a human utter a phrase like this referring to Allah or Buddha. They appears to be a kind of god humans use for placing responsibility and blame on rather than simply worshipping.

You may use this to your advantage when in need of diverting the blame for something you did. Being quick with exclaiming things like "They've drunk up all the vodka again!" should get you off the hook more effectively than most excuses.

~

The Church of Entitlement

Entitlement is a popular human belief stipulating that one should be entitled to certain rights as a reward for simply existing. One of the main holy scriptures of this religion is the Declaration of Human Rights. Unlike the general galactic meaning of the term "human rights", which mostly concerns acceptable cage sizes and transportation distances on the way to slaughterhouses, the terrestrial version is a lot more demanding. Essentially, it is a utopic list of promises which, if fulfilled, would establish a state of normality that is most desired by humans. It is yet unclear which species are supposedly responsible for delivering on these promises and why, but it is clear by the title that human rights are meant to be exclusive to humans.

Unlike animal rights (a more generic form of entitlement belief similar to human rights, only with a lot fewer rights), human rights suggest that humans are unsuitable to be bred for food or industrial materials. The reason for this xenophobic hypocrisy of keeping human rights and animal rights separate is that humans do not consider themselves to be animals. They believe that their intellectual superiority over the baboons by roughly two percent makes humans so fundamentally different from all other terrestrial creatures that it qualifies them to be considered an entirely different class of species.

Believing that human rights are universally sacred is the fundament of what is known in the rest of the universe as the human Church of Entitlement. It is the primary religion in democratic societies. (Democracy is a human governance system where your stupidity level does not correlate with the level of influence society grants you.) Its followers, predominantly inhabiting the wealthiest areas of Earth's surface, are convinced that they are entitled to a range of not always easily acquired things just because they are human.

For instance, according to the scripture, each

human is entitled to life. Adhering to this command-
ment not only makes any kind of warfare extremely
inefficient, but is also completely unsustainable. As was
vividly demonstrated during infiltrator Zorn's undercover mission as the warden in a human nursing home,
a human's right to life is generally impossible to maintain for much more than a century. Having thoroughly
studied the entitlement scriptures and fearing persecu-
tion for human rights violations, Zorn applied all life
support technology available on Earth to the home's
inhabitants, who were increasingly insistent on dying
with every additional year of life. The great infiltrator
had to abandon post when he had run out of organ
transplants, defibrillators and aphrodisiacs. One of his
wards died shortly after, aged 154, due to his body
rejecting the aardvark brain transplant Zorn had
managed to acquire when arduously pillaging the local
zoo for parts from less entitled species.

Another paradoxical right humans consider themselves entitled to is the right to security. Claiming this
right while living on one of the most insecure inhabited
planets in the galaxy is challenging in itself – especially
given that the main threat against humans typically
comes from other humans, most of whom are inherently dangerous and quite reluctant to ensure the safety
of others.

One more famous article in the human rights scripture forbids torture, cruelty and inhuman treatment of
others. The true meaning of this article has been a
matter of great debate among galactic humanologists on

how our infiltrators should tackle this principle in order to appear genuinely human. Prohibiting inhuman treatment alongside of cruelty and torture suggests that the only kind of treatment allowed should be human, which is hardly imaginable without cruelty and torture. It is widely known across the galaxy that cruelty and torture are among the most defining habits of the human species. Yet you will undoubtedly notice that humans are generally blankly unaware of this. They tend to label all sorts of brutal savagery as "inhuman" – as if any other species had ever been encountered building torture chambers and concentration camps.

Yet another right the followers of the Church of Entitlement consider themselves entitled to is privacy. Naturally, our surveillance of humans would be considered a violation of this right, which is why we have to operate in secret. This right is also keenly violated by virtually all human intelligence services that can afford paper cups and strings. However, the greatest violations of human privacy are said to be committed by gods. In fact, according to the Christian scriptures, God seems to have violated just about every human right there is. Oddly, most of the followers of the Church of Entitlement are also Christians (the Church of Entitlement is a non-exclusive church), and not a single one has ever been on record trying to file a complaint against their god for human rights violations.

Apart from the general human rights, followers of the Church of Entitlement also tend to feel entitled to additional types of rights, the most bizarre of which are the so called consumer rights. These are believed to have been granted to every human who has the habit of consuming planetary resources (i.e. any human who isn't dead or firmly determined to die of thirst and starvation) and are sometimes attributed to a sub-cult of the Church of Entitlement known as the Church of Consumerism.

Consumer rights are there to ensure that humans can keep consuming the living matter of their planet in a safe manner, are provided a sufficient choice of non-renewable resources, are able to voice their discontent when a processed piece of the planet doesn't work as advertised and have additional planetary resources expended in order to correct the dysfunction.

~

The Church of Victimhood

Ever since humanity emerged as the greatest threat to terrestrial life since the Galactic Operations Department's Terrestrial Solar Park Project (effectively discontinued once it had been discovered that the British Isles had been accidentally omitted from the average atmospheric clarity ratio calculation), countless species have fallen victim to its spread across the planet. Notably, a surprisingly large share of humanity's victims are actually human. Most were viciously killed, forcibly fertilised, deprived of their property, humiliated, forced to labour without reward, displaced, have had the wrong pronouns applied to them or have been banned from social platforms for deliberately applying the wrong pronouns to others. And while humans still deny a large share of their atrocities, they seem to be increasingly inclined to acknowledge more and more fellow humans as victims of their own or other humans' misdeeds.

Of course, to most sentient species such acknowledgement would have no significance whatsoever, as any damage that may have warranted it will have already been irreversibly applied. Humans, on the other hand, appear to find the acknowledgement of other humans' victimhood immensely valuable and tend to be very generous in victimising others at every given opportunity.

Infiltrator Zorn has put a lot of effort into researching the cause of this remarkable social phenomenon. His findings point firmly to a systemic contradiction between, on the one hand, the fact that humans are inherently greedy and selfish – and, on the other hand, their stubborn unwillingness to be perceived as such.

As a human, all it takes to be perceived as compassionate and charitable is to aid someone who has fallen victim to some horrible atrocity at the expense of one's own wealth and comfort. The problem with that is that it is only easy if you actually *are* a compassionate and charitable creature. If you, instead, happen to be human – then you are likely to perceive charitability as a bit of an uphill effort.

Had it not been so, world hunger would have long been eradicated on this planet. All orphaned children would have immediately been adopted, all elderly humans had all had someone to take care of them, all troubled teenagers from unprivileged families would have been taught proper manners, tutored, sponsored and ushered into university and no war veteran would have ever had to beg for a living. To most humans, however, sharing their wealth with unfamiliar humans or endangering the safety of their own kin by bringing home teenage convicts for positive reconditioning, is way too high of a price for having a charitable reputation.

Extending real aid to real victims is simply too expensive for most specimens of this species. Therefore, there is an immense demand among humans for cheap victims who need minimal maintenance, towards whom charitability can be extended with minimal personal sacrifice – or none at all.

This desire to earn virtue at no personal expense is the foundation of the Church of Victimhood. It is usually achieved by means of virtue signalling, which is a method commonly used by socially privileged humans to elevate themselves above less privileged ones by delegating the responsibility for the misfortunes of the latter to society as a whole, thereby allowing the responsibility to effectively dissolve in the absence of clear ownership.

This elevation is achieved by assigning a kind of certified victimhood status to humans who have suffered various misfortunes and injustices, which gives them access to a set of pre-defined privileges, thereby ensuring that the victimhood of the aforementioned individuals is well-entrenched in their identity and perfectly visible to anyone who might otherwise mistake them for fully self-sufficient humans.

The cost of these privileges is absorbed by all segments of human society – including the ones whom these privileges are supposed to benefit, while the virtue generated as a result goes to the usually already privileged humans who are most skilled in virtue signalling. Moreover, additional virtue points can be earned by shaming other privileged individuals for not sufficiently honouring the right of victimised humans to their victimhood benefits.

For the solidity with which this supposed belief in the inherent infallibility of the victim is enshrined into the fabric of human society and the fanatic devotion with which the victim's social benefits are honoured even with regard to humans who are long dead, the Galactic Theology Centre has qualified this peculiar reverence as a religion.

As an infiltrator, you may use this to your advantage and try to reap the benefits of victimhood by becoming the victim of as many misfortunes as possible and making everyone around you aware of it.

The easiest way to acquire victimhood status is to assume an unpopular belief or trait, for which you are likely to be harassed by many enough humans for you to qualify as a victim. There is, however, a bit of a catch here. Human victimisation always comes with a delay. Usually – a generation or two, but sometimes up to a couple of centuries. It appears that humans will only acknowledge your victimhood provided that whatever it is that you have been harassed or disadvantaged for is no longer unpopular.

This was clearly illustrated in the case of witches. Witches are human females with a rather terrible character and slightly unorthodox dressing habits, often skilled in using primitive sanitation equipment as means of aerial transportation. Witches were extremely unpopular during a period in human history when sanitation equipment was scarce and its misuse was considered highly provocative.

During this period many witches (and other women with an extravagant hat taste) were used as fuel for heating up the Earth atmosphere – something that is considered highly abusive if you are a human. Yet, at the time, very few humans would have acknowledged witches as victims, as was empirically proven by infiltrator Zorn in a rare experiment where the attitudes of the cheering mob were measured before and after Zorn's human host body was burned. Naturally, the great infiltrator made sure to evacuate himself through an emergency beam right before the burning – an action that was mistakenly interpreted by humans as proof of burning being effective in evicting Satan from possessed human bodies and accidentally spawned a genocidal wave which later became known as the Salem Witch Trials.

In later days, when sanitation equipment had become more affordable and more convenient aerial transportation means than a wooden stick with a truss of straws mounted on it became widely available, the public opinion towards witches gradually shifted. Presenting yourself as a witch still doesn't grant you any additional popularity, but neither does it immediately inspire other humans to mount you on a pole and burn you. On the contrary, having been burned for being a witch now elicits expressions of genuine sympathy and a disposition to trivialise your irresponsible aerial manoeuvres and your dismemberment of reptiles and insects as cultural misunderstandings.

Due to the aforementioned delay, if you wish to maximise your victimhood benefits, picking a human host identity that has already been victimised is a poor choice. Many alien infiltrators who haven't read the latest edition of this book often suffer disappointment after having picked a host body based on racial, sexual or other biological characteristics and realising that victimhood is no longer easily achievable by high skin pigmentation, having a permanent body malfunction or being persistent in exclusively performing procreational rituals with specimens of a sex that makes procreation impossible. These characteristics are simply no longer that unpopular and it is becoming increasingly hard to get humans to abuse you for possessing them.

The same applies to unpopular beliefs. Historically, beliefs for which you would be most likely to be harassed were beliefs about Earth being a sphere, about humans being descendants of prehistoric primates or the belief in universal rights for all humans. If you haven't managed to get harassed for holding any of these, it is too late to try now. They are not unpopular anymore.

Today, you are a lot more likely to be harassed for believing the opposite. Believing that races and sexes are fundamentally different and shouldn't be mixed is an opinion you are likely to get a lot of heat for today, so make sure to express that when you infiltrate. Once these beliefs have become dominant again (as all things with humans are cyclical – they most probably will), you will become the object of reverence for having held them before they were cool. You may even get financially compensated for the socio-economic disadvantages, discrimination and marginalisation you will have been subjected to by the human majority only for being a racist homophobic misogynist.

∾

Limitations of Freedom

Regardless of any given human religion's model of explaining away the everlasting existence of the universe, its practical implementation in daily human life usually boils down to various ways of limiting a human's freedom. Different human religions offer different sets of restrictions to the way humans are expected to go about their lives. There are so many of them and so few of them make any sense that you are strongly recommended to adhere to all of them indiscriminately – just to be on the safe side. We will further explain the restrictions to individual freedom you are most likely to be subjected to when trying to be respectful of religion.

One generic restriction shared by most religions is the restriction of one's freedom to kill other humans. Given the mortality of humans and their often unbearably poor sense of humour, resisting the temptation to violate this restriction will be one of your biggest challenges during infiltration. Whenever the temptation becomes unbearable – just remind yourself that the human in question is about to die anyway very soon, at least by galactic standards.

Another generic restriction regards non-consensual deprivation of property. Apparently, human gods are very particular about adhering to the basics of proprietary capitalism. This restriction should be quite easy to maintain as very few things humans possess would be of any real value anywhere else in the universe.

Most human religions will significantly limit your freedom of appearance. As already explained, humans are ashamed of their hideous bodies and strongly despise seeing the bodies of others, which is why they impose upon each other the necessity of wrapping their bodies into various rags before appearing in public. It appears that their gods share this sentiment too. Some human gods are believed to be particularly disgusted by human female bodies and prefer them to be completely covered to a point where it becomes impossible to tell that they are females.

If when infiltrating an area where one of these gods enjoys a large following, and you find yourself unsure about the sex of your human body, then you would be safer by preventively covering your whole body, including your head and face. Should you ever be confronted about your outfit being unfit for your gender, age, religious affiliation, epoch or location – play the carnival card. A carnival is an event where humans, for reasons we do not yet understand, wear things they would never wear otherwise. Say that you are on your way to a carnival, and humans will leave you alone, regardless of what you are wearing (as long as you are wearing *something*).

There are a few outfits this may not work well with, like when infiltrator Zorn waited a couple of decades too long with premiering the parade uniform he'd acquired at a great discount from a deeply depressed human he abducted from a Berlin bunker in 1945.

Some human religions restrict the human's ability to use certain other mammals as fuel. Most commonly that mammal is a pig. We aren't sure why that is, but since pigs are the most human-like mammals you will find on Earth, this restriction is most likely a precaution against accidental cannibalism. They may not strike you as the type, but humans consider cannibalism to be a shameful practice. So shameful, in fact, that even if stranded on a deserted island with no other available sources of fuel but another human who is entirely useless for anything else but fuel, for the reason of being dead, most humans would rather put that accompanying dead human body underground and allow it to rot away while they themselves slowly starve to death.

For this reason, most humans who do practise cannibalism do it exclusively with themselves, eating away a couple pounds each year by discretely biting off bits of their own fingernails when nobody else is watching. Because this behaviour usually manifests itself when the human is under stress, some scholars have suggested that it might be a defence instinct: in order to avoid being eaten by an approaching larger predator, the targeted humans will try to quickly eat themselves so that there is nothing left by the time the predator catches up with them. Not the most rational instinct, perhaps, but no less rational than the human instinct of wetting oneself when threatened or the instinct of stretching one's facial muscles whenever faced with a camera.

The most important restriction religious humans have to live with regards their ability to question the religion itself. Religious followers are very keen on imposing this restriction upon everyone else, thereby making any external aid in recognising how misguided their understanding of the world is virtually impossible.

RELIGIOUS RITUALS

Do not expect to be able to comprehend the logic of human religion when infiltrating Earth. It is impossible because there seldom is any logic involved in the first place. The important thing is that you learn the basics of human religious rituals and codes, so that you can restrain yourself from acting as any reasonable sentient creature would if entangled in one. We will here go through the basics of those human religious rituals that are most likely to provoke you into compromising action if you aren't properly aware of their mechanics.

Praying

Humans have been out of touch with the rest of the universe ever since Earth was muted and banned for spamming all telepathic communication frequencies with annoyingly repetitive messages. The messages were thought to be DDOS attacks on the Galactic Operations Department's telepathic receptors until our humanologists discovered the human ritual of praying.

Praying is a human method of persuasion targeted at a god who, however just, almighty, all-seeing and all-loving, is expected to be reluctant to intervene in inter-human matters unless repeatedly nagged at. Prayer is an odd human form of nagging that is rarely structured as a convincing sales pitch or a well-founded courtroom appeal, but mostly consists of learned verses stating the assumed remote whereabouts of the praying human's father, his level of greatness and various well-wishes to his name and the approach of his kingdom, repeated over and over.

As prayer doesn't really require any substantial effort apart from learning verses and suffering the monotony of one's own repetitive chanting, much of the time humans could have spent attempting to acquire things they desire is spent praying for a god to provide them.

The seeming ease of achieving results by simply babbling predefined lines of speech in one's head has spawned an inflation of praying. As humans with rivalling interests are quite aware of each other's equal chances of swaying a god in one's favour through prayer, they eventually tend to go down the beaten path of trying to out-pray each other. They pray longer, more often and even ask others to pray for them, ultimately creating an overwhelming noise that jams all other telepathic communication.

We haven't yet seen any causality between praying and the events unrolling in favour of the praying human, but every time these things coincide humans are quick to assume the prayer has worked. When the events do not turn out the way the praying human wishes, the most common human conclusion is that they should have prayed more. Both conclusions work in favour of using prayer as a method of achieving goals which otherwise would have required some actual work in order to be achieved.

Going to Church

Churches are usually large and eccentric constructions, the design of which provides very few clues as to their purpose. They commonly feature high rocket shaped domes and equally frightening rocket shaped windows, made from a material that effectively obscures every-thing that goes on inside. The outer walls often have shapes of monstrous creatures sticking out of them, most of which are even more monstrous than humans. Some believe these to be prototypes of hypothetical species which could have come to be had humans been able to cross-breed with other mammals.

For a time, churches were believed to be rocket assembly facilities, but the closest thing to a rocket any of our expeditions has ever encountered inside those rocket-shaped domes were small hollow metallic shells dangling from the dome's ceiling. The shells are equipped with long ropes, which humans appear to enjoy pulling. So much, in fact, that they would climb hundreds of stairs only to pull at that rope a dozen times before climbing down again.

Churches are designed to accommodate a number of religious rituals. Here humans perform the water-proofing tests of their offspring by submerging them into liquid under the strict supervision of a human whose profession is known for its strong affection for children. It is also here that couples of humans promise each other not to couple with other humans, which is said to please their god immensely. But the most common human ritual a church is designed to house is the ritual of going to it.

Contrary to what the wording suggests, the going part is the most insignificant component of the ritual. The main component is *being* in church and enduring everything that goes on there, which happens to be exhaustingly little. What usually does go on is something humans call "service", but which is something very few truly service-minded creatures would refer to as such. Very little concern is extended to ensuring the comfort of visitors during church service and the only refreshments or snacks ever served have a disturbingly cannibalistic character.

The true purpose of churches has long been a matter of great debate among galactic humanologists. Once the rocket assembly facility theory was discarded, observational studies advanced the theory of churches being a place of collective prayer. Critics of this theory pointed to the utter pointlessness of constructing expensive buildings only to house an activity that can be easily exercised anywhere at any time.

The collective prayer theory was finally discarded after observational studies by means of remote brain scan technology revealed that only a small fraction of the time in church is actually devoted to prayer. Half of it appears to be spent on pondering things completely unrelated to religion, one quarter is spent on sneak peeking at other humans, ten percent is spent on thinking of a clever way of placing an embarrassingly small bill in the offering cup without anyone noticing and the rest is spent on trying to not fall asleep.

The fact that the noise-oscillating assemblies of children in church is male-only has briefly spawned some speculation about whether church service could be some sort of savage rite of passage into manhood, but evidence soon proved that there was nothing more elaborate to it but the mere sexual preference of the clergy.

After centuries of observation it was finally established that churches are, in fact, a clever combination of hibernation chambers and training facilities, where humans are trained in hibernating with their eyes open – a skill much appreciated when defending a planet against invaders that never sleep.

Eating Prophets

There have been accounts of religious rituals in multiple places in our galaxy. Only a few of them had cannibalistic and vampirical elements (all of them on Earth). There is, however, only one known religion in the universe whose followers are expected to eat their own prophet. In religious temples all across the planet human priests feed worshipers with pieces of their prophet's body and encourage them to chase the pieces down with a sip of the prophet's blood.

Despite having only one prophet, in two thousand years this religion has managed to establish itself as the largest one on the planet. This exceptional growth has many possible explanations, but with a species as gluttonous and prone to occasional famine as humans, feeding your worshipers clearly provides a strong competitive advantage.

Initially, this growth was inhibited by the natural scarcity of the prophet's body and its diminishing nutritiousness in the absence of proper refrigeration equipment. But then the clergy managed to convince its followers who, like most humans, had a very limited understanding of human anatomy, that their prophet was in fact made of bread and wine. This rather exotic notion faced little opposition from the followers, most of whom much preferred bread and wine to chewing on centuries old human cadavers. It was also endorsed by financial institutions and eagerly sponsored by the Mediterranean Vineyard and Bakery Association.

If you are to partake in this ritual, be sure to only eat bread and wine offered by the priest. Don't try to bring your own – even if you find the rations too small. Also, please mind that nowadays this ritualistic cannibalism is exclusively imaginary. Humans never eat the real prophet anymore. Many human clerics believe that they do – despite being fully aware of having extracted what they claim to be the flesh of their prophet from a plastic package decorated with cow depictions, which one of the choir boys had purchased at the supermarket earlier and brought to the church as an atonement for having been very naughty. However, sometimes humans bring dead people into their churches and pray around them. It is easy to assume these to be dead prophets. They are not. Don't eat them.

Offerings and Sacrifice

While many humans practise their daily religious worship by publicly exposing their prophets' most vulnerable moments (like hanging half-naked on a cross and bleeding to death), some use similarly unfavourable depictions of their prophets as a signal event for grand scale offering rituals – sometimes involving human sacrifice.

Typically, the signal event that initiates such rituals is a depiction or mention of a prophet in an amusing context. The more amusing the context, the greater the ritualistic sacrifice. Rituals where the signal event is a rather unamusing depiction of the prophet having a Piña Colada on the beach usually only involve non-human sacrifice – typically offerings by fire of inanimate things, such as dust bins, national flags and vehicles (preferably those belonging to other humans or those used for law enforcement). Grand scale rituals that involve human sacrifice, on the other hand, typically begin with much more entertaining prophet illustrations.

If such a signal event happens when you are operating undercover as a human who is expected to worship the unfavourably depicted prophet, the protocol is to go to the source of the depiction and yell profanities mixed with religious mantra until law enforcement arrives. At this point, the offering begins with heavy objects you collect at the spot and sacrifice by throwing them at the law enforcement officers. If you see the human policemen step back from their vehicles, it is likely a signal to initiate the next offering phase: fire sacrifice of the vehicles. This phase usually concludes the ritual, but in rituals where the prophet illustrations are particularly amusing, you may also need to sacrifice some humans by means of gunfire, bombs or ritualistic clubbing to death. Do not be discouraged by the seeming reluctance with which the humans are being sacrificed. We have observed multiple religious human rituals of this kind and they always involve sacrificing reluctant humans.

It is important to ensure that you have accurately identified the signal event before you engage in this ritual. The most common rookie mistake is to mix up the prophets. The prophet that needs to be depicted for the ritual to start is a bearded male in a robe and a pouchy headdress. Inconveniently enough, most human prophets happen to have been bearded males in robes, so the headdress is extremely important. On one of his missions, infiltrator Zorn managed to sacrifice a whole fleet of human police vehicles after receiving a postcard with a depiction of a bearded man in a robe transported in a most entertaining way by means of an airborne vehicle propelled by non-flying mammals. He failed to notice that the man's headdress wasn't pouchy. Pouchiness is key.

. . .

Christmas

Many alien infiltrators have reported a sequence of paranormal changes in the most human-infested areas of the planet, which consistently occur at the end of each cycle Earth makes around its sun. It begins with a gradual change of sonic ambience in places humans frequent. Then mysterious tree cadavers begin to appear everywhere, human males begin dressing in a very unorthodox fashion, consumption goes through the roof and just when it all culminates into a bizarre frenzy of total madness – it suddenly subsides and in a week or two everything goes back to normal again.

If this happens when you are on your mission – don't panic. This is called Christmas, and it makes for a convenient opportunity to exceed your abduction targets.

Christmas is a birthday celebration in honour of one of our early infiltrators, who accidentally started the Christian religion when trying to explain away his use of extraterrestrial fish cloning and death curing technology to impress humans and whom they later attached to an installation made of tree cadavers in the most ungentle way.

Unlike other human birthday celebrations, which normally feature a cake and balloons, Christmas is more strongly characterised by destruction of trees. In the advent of Christmas, humans across large parts of the planet go out into the woods, chop down millions of trees, drag them into their homes, hang hollow balls onto their limbs and then watch them slowly die while singing merry songs. The total death toll amounts to around two hundred million trees every year, of which a hundred and twenty million suffer the aforementioned slow and humiliating death inside the human habitat and the remaining eighty million are simply burned because no human wanted to buy them.

We are not sure about the pretext of this annual tree massacre, but many suspect that this resentment towards trees has something to do with that cross they nailed agent Yeshua to having been made of wood. Humans are exceptionally talented at placing the blame for everything they do on someone else. That would also explain why they send thin slices of dead trees to each other as a reminder of Christmas, despite their perfect access to many non-destructive means of communication. (The same kind of logic can be observed in another annual mass-murder event practised by humans in some parts of the planet. In this case, the victim is not a tree, but a turkey – a creature so alienly beautiful some humans have even named their country after it. This annual human mass-murder of turkeys is called "Thanksgiving" and is believed to be a sarcastic metaphor suggesting retribution for some terrible misdeeds supposedly committed by turkeys in the past.)

The Christmas retribution against trees further continues when humans wrap various useless items into sheets made out of dead trees and put them underneath their very own tree carcass for their children to find and tear apart.

Beyond all of this morbid savagery, Christmas actually has two large benefits to us. Firstly, all this chopping, wrapping and burning is really helpful in increasing the planet temperature, and if this goes on, Earth should very soon be warm enough to colonise. Secondly, it offers some excellent abduction opportunities thanks to a very convenient lie humans tell their offspring. The lie is that on the night before Christmas, a bearded man in a full body costume is to enter their habitat at night to add some items wrapped in tree remains to the ones already underneath the tree carcass.

Somehow, the prospect of this event gets human children overwhelmed with excitement. On any other night, such an intrusion would cause human parents serious concerns about the safety of their young, but on Christmas human children are rather instructed to stay quietly in bed all night no matter what. Neither does the common human parental advice to their children not to sit in the lap of strange men apply on Christmas. If you have never felt you had a good chance to safely abduct some human children, Christmas would definitely be it.

Easter

Easter is a day when humans paint boiled bird embryos to commemorate infiltrator Yeshua's ascension back to the mothership after his aforementioned near-death experience with a wooden cross. The embryos are allegedly delivered to humans by a hyper-potent lagomorph for purposes which cannot conceivably be other than malign, but which our scientists haven't been able to connect to the commemorated event in any sensible way.

The ascension event itself seems to have made a lasting impression on humans – as has infiltrator Yeshua's public torment. There have been shows in human history which have drawn larger crowds of spectators, but no other event has spawned an equally unceasing demand for souvenirs – for millennia to come. Apparently, humans not only found seeing our agent being nailed to a piece of wood very entertaining – they also found it tremendously useful. Life saving, in fact. Our records show that while his hands were being nailed to the cross, Yeshua made some emotional exclamations about the humans standing by, whom he blamed for his unfortunate situation. As it often is with humans, they only heard what they wanted to hear. His phrase "I'm dying here for your sins, you sinners!" (the original wording was changed to better fit family audiences) was interpreted as if Yeshua willingly absolved all humans of their sins by dying a terrible death.

This was, of course, warmly welcomed as it basically meant that humans could now start sinning again from a clean slate. Few bothered to ponder the exact mechanics of such a transaction. When confronted with the question, human clerics usually claim that God, who is known for his inclination to correct repeated human misconduct through mass extermination, was persuaded not to do so this time, but rather accept the sacrifice of his son being brutally murdered as compensation. (Complicated Father-Son relationships are quite common in the Christian scriptures.)

Coincidentally, our operative Yeshua is believed to be that son, and is also the one who is claimed to have suggested this bargain in the first place. Why any father would have found such a trade favourable is one of many questions to which human clerics respond that their lord works in mysterious ways. This statement of the obvious is something human clerics do every time their god fails them.

Funerals

Humans hate each other so much that whenever one dies, the ones closest to them tend to throw a celebration, during which they jointly enjoy watching the body of the dead human being disposed of in a most solemn manner. The body is usually packed into an expensive wooden cask (probably in order to best preserve its qualities and add characteristic flavour during the ageing process) and submerged into a pit deep enough to ensure that the human will not be able to escape in the unlikely event of them not being completely dead. In order to add some additional solemnity to this celebration of death, more commonly known as a "funeral", humans mutilate a large number of plants, arrange their reproductive parts in large wreaths, which they leave around the dead human's place of disposal to slowly decay and rot away together with the human.

Funerals are about as fun as any human ritual gets. You will never find a larger number of constantly apologising humans in any other place. Humans are generally really bad at admitting their wrongs, but during a funeral they all suddenly seem to go out of their way to make it abundantly clear how sorry they are. Apologies are so plentiful during a funeral that it sometimes is hard to tell what each human is so sorry for. Beginner infiltrators often assume (quite understandably) that an apology about a human's death is a confession of murder. The multiple police investigations initiated by infiltrators after having received such apologies at funerals have shown that that is very rarely the case. Most likely the apologies regard the lies immediately following the apology about what a wonderful person the deceased human was.

Lying about any positive traits the dead human could have had and concealing all the evidently negative ones is the primary conversation subject of any funeral. Every such lie seems to greatly upset the humans who were most affected by the deceased human's wickedness due to cohabitation and ancestry, sometimes provoking uncontrollable outbursts of incredibly annoying sounds and facial flux. This is something you will have to learn to tolerate. As infiltrator Zorn's multiple funeral experiments have made clear, attempts to remedy the human's distress by offsetting all the preposterous lies with an accurate description of the deceased human's horribly disgraceful nature are unlikely to produce a more tolerable human behaviour.

Due to all this constant lying and sobbing, the atmosphere at funerals tends to get quite gloomy. However much this may depress your working environment, multiple experiments have shown that all the known ways of trying to cheer humans up are of very little use when applied at funerals. Jokes and puns appear to be very divisive, provoking outbursts of rage to humans suddenly departing from the funeral while covering up their faces with the extremities of their appendages and making grunting sounds. Even the most certain method of lifting a human's spirit – poking the human on the sides – has shown to perform poorly at funerals. In a report from one of his experiments, infiltrator Zorn stated that out of the over two hundred humans he had poked on the sides during a burial ceremony, only three exhibited observable signs of an improved mood. As the autopsy of their bodies later showed, two of them suffered from severe personality disorders long before lethal force was applied to their heads multiple times by other attendants of the funeral.

≈

The Purpose of Religion

Religious behaviour has been encountered many times before among various primitive civilisations across the universe. It usually ceases after sufficient discoveries within physics, chemistry and astronomy are made known to the populace. With humans, however, the correlation between scientific enlightenment and religious beliefs seems to be less linear. You may still encounter educated physicists and astronomers who maintain beliefs that fundamentally contradict basic laws of physics.

This inconsistency has long been blamed on the chaotic structure of the human brain, infamously known as the most disorderly information storage device in the universe. With a brain structure this messy, it is hardly surprising that two sets of information, such as the variety size of the terrestrial fauna and the logistics of bringing two specimens of each species onboard a wooden boat, may never connect. Later it has been discovered that the human gravitation towards religion stems from something else entirely.

Our scholars recently learned that humans use religion as a source of something few other species have any need of, but which to humans seems to be of utmost existential importance: purpose.

Purpose (often confused with a porpoise – a large aquatic mammal, whose adorably cute squeaking and hopping about the sea surface quite suffices in justifying this planet's existence), is the human notion of their own existence being a part of some deliberate plan that goes beyond their parents' plan of becoming parents. Although it is a well-established fact that all humans who have ever lived eventually ended up as fertiliser, many humans still struggle to understand their purpose on Earth. Even when this rather obvious purpose is explained to them they seem to always want another, as if simply existing weren't legitimate without proper justification.

Religion has miraculously survived among humans throughout their evolution thanks to religious authorities always adapting to scientific revelations by skilfully changing their story to make it compatible with the improved understanding of reality. But the main reason for its exceptional endurance is that to humans the story of a religion has always been secondary to its purpose. And the purpose of all human religions has always been the same: purpose itself.

As long as you keep purpose intact, you can feed religious humans virtually any story and they will believe it. This was empirically proven by infiltrator Zorn when he, working undercover as a catholic priest, managed to deliver multiple sermons where he read passages from the Quran, the Book of Mormon and the Book of Lucifer verbatim, only replacing all the names with biblical ones, without any noticeable reaction from the congregation. It wasn't until his seventy-second sermon, where Zorn was reading passages from *Winnie the Pooh*, that one woman in the congregation wondered whether eating all that honey and getting stuck in the hole was Jesus' way of sacrificing himself for the sins of mankind or whether feeding honey to Jesus was Judas' deliberate method of betrayal.

So, what is it with purpose that makes it so addictive to humans? You may ask. Humans have long been considered one of the most useless species in the universe, but the current oversupply of natural fertiliser on their planet has taken their uselessness to a point where their mere existence has become a sheer inconvenience to just about everyone else. To their great disadvantage, human intellect – albeit extremely primitive – is just advanced enough for most of them to realise the utter pointlessness of everything they do. Humans are really good at keeping themselves busy throughout their lives, but sooner or later this realisation catches up with most of them.

Most species would find it a relief – a good excuse to stop doing things and simply focus on enjoying existence. Humans, however, are incapable of simply being. As was stated earlier, humans are addicted to doing. But they are also reluctant to admit that the purpose of all their doings is doing itself. And since almost no human activity ever sustains more than three consecutive repetitions of the question "Why?", humans eagerly adopt the notion of a divine plan that involves every living creature as a handy substitute for the real purpose they are hopelessly incapable of devising for themselves.

An important perk many human religions provide their followers with in the absence of any real purpose is the illusion of immortality. Human science hasn't yet advanced far enough to be able to halt the gradual decay of the human body (and for the sake of all galactic life it hopefully never will), which essentially means that the average human life is nothing but a short sprint towards certain death, much of which is plagued with anxiety in anticipation of the inevitable end. Most terrestrial creatures dislike dying, but humans are particularly uneasy about it. This makes humans very receptive to a variety of bizarre ideas about continued sentient existence beyond the boundaries of one's mortal body.

The idea itself is, of course, perfectly sane given that most intelligent species in the universe have advanced to non-physical existence, without which our undercover operations on Earth would have been much harder to sustain. But unlike us, humans are nowhere close to developing such technologies. Instead, many of them believe that dying means becoming an invisible version of yourself with retained cognitive abilities and a great enthusiasm for pranks.

Religion takes this notion one step further. Major human religions promise those who obediently suffer all the inconveniences dictated by their god throughout their lives a ticket to heaven right after death. As mentioned earlier, heaven is what human religious scriptures call everything that surrounds Earth. In other words, dead humans are promised to be sent into space. This is, of course, complete shenanigans, but as this supposed space launch is said to only regard the non-physical part of the human, failure to deliver on this promise is impossible for humans to verify.

Why the opportunity to be sent out into the empty vacuum of space without a physical body should motivate a human to live a life of austerity and fierce suppression of basic instincts we do not know. Some attribute it to the relativity factor: endlessly floating through the emptiness of space might come as a great relief in comparison with the life one would have had to live in order to earn this pleasure. But a more likely explanation is not so much about the attractiveness of this rather suspicious reward, but rather about the fear of the alternative.

According to major human religions, not living a life of austerity and fierce suppression of basic human instincts is a ticket to an underground place much worse than human life itself. Various human religious scriptures describe this place differently, but fire, lava and insufferably high air temperatures seem to be a recurring pattern. This suggests that the intended destination might either be somewhere at the core of the planet, or the surface of the planet a couple of centuries into the future. Either destination is technically possible, but very unlikely provided the current level of human technology, which so far is nowhere close to enabling time travel. (Although human scientists have developed a formula for time travel several decades ago, it was immediately acquired by a major oil company and never heard of since.)

Whatever it is that motivates each human to submit

their freedom to the bizarre commandments of an ancient scripture, religion does have a very important purpose for us. Without it, humans would have been a lot harder to lure into submission and would have been a lot more suspicious about accidental encounters with our 3D projections of selectable human host bodies, some of which were mistakenly equipped with wings by a rookie Plutonian model designer who clearly hadn't taken enough time to study the anatomy of land-living terrestrial mammals.

Religion also presents a great advantage to infiltrators trying to coerce a human into a desired behaviour but lacking a credible excuse for doing so. The extensiveness of human religious scriptures, the extreme ambiguity of their contents and the austerity of the human memory banks allows any infiltrator who learns the scripture by heart (an operation that shouldn't take a moderately intelligent being more than ten minutes) to extract random quotes of the relevant god and use them to motivate the desired human behaviour, excusing the seemIng contradiction between the quote and the behaviour with the mysteriousness of the aforementioned god's ways. This, apart from the free wine and the unrestricted access to many research-friendly dungeons with freshly deceased human subjects conveniently placed in them, is the main reason why most of our infiltrators work undercover as priests.

Zorn search party telepathic intercom transmission excerpt 6

Transmitted one minute and seventeen seconds after the second dispatch.

Balbooza: [*Gee, was this... Was this in the manual?*]
Gee: [*No. It most definitely wasn't.*]
Balbooza: [*So... Have you got any idea about what it is we are looking at?*]
Gee: [*I think it might be a human skeleton.*]
Balbooza: [*What's that?*]
Gee: [*It is what the human body is built around.*]
Balbooza: [*Is it supposed to jump out of the ground like this and make these unsettling noises?*]
Gee: [*I don't believe human skeletons are expected to do that, no.*]
Balbooza: [*Then why—*]
Gee: [*Dispatcher, you were asked to beam us to the darkest and least populated place in Disneyland. [Intercom transmission] Well, then how come there are screaming human cadavers jumping at us here? **Intercom transmission** Oh, I see.*]
Balbooza: [*What did she say?*]
Gee: [*She said that they don't register on the plasma scanner, so they cannot be real human cadavers.*]
Balbooza: [*Why would fake human cadavers jump out of the ground and scream at people?*]
Gee: [*I don't know. Probably for the same reason that*

this low quality hologram is wobbling in front of the annoyingly slow-moving vehicle we are being trans-ported by. It's clearly human made and humans never make any sense. Come on, let's get out of this thing and find a place where Zorn has the best chance of spotting us. With all this smoke and gloom this "Haunted Mention" – or whatever the dispatcher said it's called – clearly isn't that sort of place.]

Chapter 7

Human Science and Technology

This is the shortest chapter in the book, because by all galactic standards human science and technology really do not amount to very much and will likely not be of much help during your infiltration mission. After many millennia of stubbornly attributing everything that goes on around them to the malevolence of various immaterial deities (often inspired by the comic strips infiltrator Zorn left on cave walls during his wait for excavation after having prematurely taken to his ion blaster in an attempt to divert the unhealthy attention of a deaf bat), humans have only recently figured out that their body cells consist of atoms, which are systems of spherical particles revolving around atomic cores. They have also figured out that the Solar system consists of spherical bodies revolving around a core spherical star. Yet, for some reason, they still haven't made the connection between these two facts.

Humans are, therefore, completely unaware of the fact that their galaxy is just one of several billion cells which together constitute one of the rather extravagant tail tips of a three-tailed luminous jelly tortoise. You would be wise not to try to enlighten them on this matter, as any knowledge that does not put the human species at the centre of everything always seems to depress them, and you will find that depressed humans are a great deal more annoying than regular ones.

As you may already have realised, you will be dealing with a species with a very low level of scientific development. It is a species that builds robots with the sole purpose of behaving like humans instead of being useful. It is a species that still uses inflatable vests as the only available type of safety equipment onboard its passenger aircraft – despite having invented a primitive but functional parachuting technology and despite the overwhelming evidence that the cushioning effect of an inflatable vest is very limited when crashing into a rock at 800 kilometres per hour. The mere fact that such a primitive creature can be allowed to pilot aircraft without the assistance of artificial intelligence is something our infiltrators always find extremely entertaining. You can easily identify other undercover aliens as the ones clapping their hands after their aeroplane has landed. Most humans legitimately frown at this behaviour, but it can hardly be helped. It is just incredibly impressive to see a human manage to land a flying machine without crashing.

Of the few useful things humans have ever created, most were initially designed to harm other humans, but were eventually repurposed due to unsatisfactory results. Humans initially invented computers to calculate ballistic trajectories, but have managed to repurpose them for controlling themselves. Nuclear power plants were an unexpected spin-off from a rather successful attempt to create a weapon capable of destroying the whole planet. Microwave ovens were initially meant to work as army radars, but kept blowing up the military staff's lunchboxes and are now one of the most entertaining demolition tools for anything that fits into them.

We believe that toilet seats were initially intended to function as chair traps. If placed out casually in the wilderness, they would lure enemies to rest on them – only to suddenly suck the victim in and flush them down a sewage pipeline. This ground-breaking theory was first introduced by infiltrator Zorn in his evacuation report, explaining why him being stuck in a human sewer for a week had absolutely nothing to do with the penny he had accidentally dropped down the drain earlier. There is yet no other documented evidence supporting this theory available, but the Galactic Board of Fringe Sciences has unanimously approved this theory of Zorn as the most scientifically convincing one in the absence of any other theories on the origins of human toilet seat technology.

Just as the primary purpose of human existence is destruction and depletion of planetary resources, the purpose of most human technological advancement is to increase the pace and scale of such destruction and depletion.

In the early days of human civilization there were only a few human settlements, the inhabitants of which rarely bothered to annoy the other settlements by defiling them with their presence. The impact of each settlement on the surrounding flora and fauna was then only limited to the consumption needs of that settlement's population, the size of which was kept reasonably stable thanks to terrestrial bacteria, poisonous vegetation, carnivorous mammals, venomous snakes and the inherent urge of human males to prove their bravery to females. Over time, humans discovered that they could deplete a lot more of the surrounding flora and fauna by utilising the consumption capacity of the other settlements. This was the beginning of a phenomenon humans call "trade", which until today remains one of the fastest methods of dramatically decreasing the life expectancy of a habitable planet known to science.

Early human trade evangelists advocated a societal structure where all human settlements would be merged into one, thereby minimising the lead time between the point when a resource is acquired and the point when it is consumed. However, very soon it became clear that a lot more resources could be depleted if humans instead spread out widely over the surface of the planet. In part, because this would allow for a more even pace of planetary surface exploitation, but mainly because distances create the need for transportation, and that would open a whole new range of ways to deplete much more of Earth's resources in various creative ways only to move something from point A to point B.

Unlike an intelligent species such as ours, which invented teleportation long before it invented the skateboard (one of the most useless inventions in the history of any ethereal species that has access to teleportation), humans really made sure to try out almost every conceivable transportation technology before they even started considering any that do not require hauling things along the planet's surface.

The numerous trails of human footprints leading straight into solid walls were earlier seen as proof of humans having discovered teleportation technology. However, a recent study has revealed that all occurrences of such footprint trails can be explained by either insobriety or mass executions. In the absence of teleportation, Earth's strong gravitation does make hauling a lot more practical than tossing shipping containers around in the air. This has provided humans with a compelling business case for reshaping the surface terrain of their planet into a vast network of uninhabitable streaks of tar-tainted soil and long metallic strain pairs mounted onto evenly cut blocks of dead vegetation. Along these strains and streaks humans would then drag various transportation vehicles, propelled primarily by burning any kind of terrestrial resource susceptible to fire.

It is no coincidence that of all the roughly seventy thousand known propellant technologies, humans have first discovered those that give them an excuse to burn things. As mentioned earlier, humans love to see things burn. You will notice that a human can sometimes sit and stare at a fire for hours out of sheer amusement, hurrying to add more burnable material to the inferno as soon as the fire begins to subside. Something that would make most creatures shiver in terror – the sight of gradual destruction and evaporation of matter by the force of a flame – gives humans a sense of comfort and calm. So much, in fact, that some humans arrange special places for burning inside their own habitat, where they can share the sight of destruction with their close ones at any moment of their choosing.

Although human scientists spend a great deal of time trying to study the remnants of the past, their insights and conclusions are almost always wrong and their research is usually misguided. There are multiple human theories on why dinosaurs went extinct and all of them are based on the I assumption that humans were the first species to have developed nuclear weapons. Humans are still trying to decipher the phrase "We should have built that wall", carved by the last neanderthal a century after humans started migrating to Europe, and they are still trying to make a storyline out of the emoji sets we left on the walls of Egyptian tombs.

To the galaxy's great relief, the human propensity to spread and infest is a lot more pronounced on Earth than it is outside it. Humans seem entirely preoccupied with exploiting their home planet. They hadn't even paid a visit to their planet's only moon until half a century ago (a visit that would have seemed entirely unremarkable if not for their ingenious secret technology that made the flag they placed on the moon's surface flap – despite the absence of both wind and atmosphere). At this pace of space exploration, we should consider ourselves fortunate not to have to expect humans to appear on any other cosmic body before the certain demise of their species is complete.

It is worth noting that the technological backwardness of the human species does not fully reflect the actual level of its scientific development. For some reason, many human scientific advances that could entirely change human society are simply never put to use. Equally, certain prehistoric human practices appear to survive and outlast just about any innovation.

It may not be entirely obvious, but quite a while ago humans developed virtual and augmented reality technology. It allows them to generate endless variations of visual environments at almost zero unit cost and only requires the human to wear a special headset, which needs to be recharged occasionally. Still, decades later we are seeing absolutely no decrease in the amount of planetary resources humans use up to alter their physical environment for purely aesthetic purposes.

Humans keep buying wallpaper and regularly

investing great amounts of time and money in refurbishing their habitat after each new whim of fashion, while only using VR headsets for recreational shooting at imaginary alien creatures in virtual worlds no sane human should want to inhabit. Many of these virtual experiences involve the most intricate visual effects, with colourful blasts of light, powerful explosions and impressively realistic imaginary creatures. Yet humans still eagerly flock to annual open gatherings to marvel at a spectacle called "fireworks", where fortunes large enough to feed a middle-sized human village in the hungrier parts of Earth for a whole generation are blown up in the air for sheer amusement.

This reluctance to make proper use of available technology can be observed all across human existence. Human scientists have developed a wide variety of strong, flexible and durable synthetic materials, but humans still build their furniture out of dead trees and animal skins. Humans have advanced far enough in robotics to be able to automatise most of their society, and yet they still prefer to let other humans scrub floors, make hamburgers and die in combat, while robots are primarily used for cheap laughs through badly impersonating humans.

Humans have invented chemical and biological weapons, which are designed only to kill humans, while keeping the surroundings intact. Not only are these surgically precise weapons seldom used, but humans have actually banned them altogether and are instead using weapons that leave a trail of devastation wherever applied.

Perhaps the most incomprehensible aversion to technology is reading. While having invented a variety of effective, cheap, secure and climate-neutral transmission methods and carriers of information, a large share of humans still prefers to consume information off remains of dead tree carcasses. Advocates of such barbaric practices usually defend this atrocity by claiming that remains of tree cadavers have a "better feel" than various types of non-organic screens. Obviously, such cynical monstrosity deserves no further comment.

For a time it was believed that humans possessed certain technologies that would make them appear more impressive in the eyes of the galactic community. For instance, repeated occurrences of the same events, attitudes and observed apparel styles had long led us to believe that humans were exercising time travel. It later became clear that such repetitions were merely a consequence of the insufficiency of human memory, the human inability to learn from one's mistakes and the cyclicity of human fashion (which is, effectively, a product of the prior two factors).

The human propensity to postpone everything enjoyable for later in life while becoming increasingly parsimonious with age had long led us to believe that humans must have discovered immortality. This belief was quite easily discarded a couple of generations later after all the observed subjects had died – most of them quite rich and extremely displeased with their life enjoyment statistics.

Today we know that during the course of their history humans have not, in fact, invented anything substantial. Most of the technological inventions that have had any substantial impact on human life were actually smuggled in by undercover aliens disguised as human scientists. The only thing humans have ever invented themselves that really made a big difference for them is god.

～

Zorn search party telepathic intercom transmission excerpt 7

Transmitted thirty-five minutes and thirteen seconds after the second dispatch.

Gee: [*Gee, when you were scanning that human's brain, did it say anything about the purpose of this Disneyland place?*]
Balbooza: [*No, it didn't. But I registered that the human had really really really wanted to come here for a long time, as did all the other humans in the juvenile care institution he spent his early life in.*]
Gee: [*Then it must be a place of great importance and prestige. I am sure it is no coincidence that the great Zorn should want to infiltrate this place.*]

Balbooza: [*So what do you think is going on here?*]

Gee: [*Well, let us think. What have we been able to observe so far?*]

Balbooza: [*According to my preliminary calculations, 92% of the humans within a five-kilometre radius are photographing themselves and their surroundings, 89% are consuming various fuel, 78% are producing endorphins, 54% are making loud noises, of which 37% are requests for a balloon...*]

Gee: [*Yes, yes, humans tend to do all of that a lot. You saw it all happen at the zoo as well. But what is different about this place?*]

Balbooza: [*Well, one observable difference is that there are no other animals here but humans.*]

Gee: [*That's right. They don't seem to allow any other species in here. There must be things here they don't want anyone else to see.*]

Balbooza: [*Also, at the zoo I haven't seen humans being tumbled around and propelled at dangerous velocities in various rotating and spinning machines. What do you suppose they are?*]

Gee: [*My first thought was that they must be some sort of torture devices. I've read about such things in Zorn's chronicles from mediaeval Spain, where he sheds a lot of light on how Christianity became the leading human religion in less than a millennium. But then I noticed the great similarity some of these machines bear to the superluminal travel simulators we were trained in before being sent to Earth...*]

Balbooza: [*Oh, so you think...*]

245

Gee: [*Look, that one over there is called* Astro Orbitor. *Why do you think that is?*]

Balbooza: [*It doesn't look very... superluminal.*]

Gee: [*That is because it's a beginner level device. See, all the humans in it are small. Now, see those spikes next to the* Space Mountain? *What do they look like to you?*]

Balbooza: [*Rockets.*]

Gee: [*They sure do. Could be a coincidence, but then there's this huge sign next to the Astro Orbitor that says* Star Tours, *and also that strange building with four large parabolic antennae right behind it, so...*]

Balbooza: [*So you think this place is some kind of space training facility? But it's huge! You said they haven't got the technology to travel anywhere further than Venus and that the furthest away from Earth they've ever been is their own moon, and even that was half a century ago and likely a scam.*]

Gee: [*That is indeed what we thought.*]

Balbooza: [*But what would they be training for? And why keep it such a secret that even our infiltrators have missed it?*]

Gee: [*I don't know. But some of the things I am seeing here are really bothering me. I don't know what Buzz Lightyear Astro Blasters are, but I don't much like the sound of it. Also, did you notice that building with the sign* Guardians of the Galaxy *down south?*]

Balbooza: [*I did. Do you think that is who they think they are? Guardians of the galaxy?*]

Gee: [*I hope not. From everything I've read of human history, every time they declare themselves the guardians* *of anything – it usually ends badly for whatever it is they are supposed to be guarding.*]

Balbooza: [*There was another building next to it called the* Avengers Headquarters *that had a suspiciously advanced looking spacecraft parked on the roof.*]

Gee: [*If these avengers have headquarters, then there must be a lot of them. So whom are they so determined to avenge that they form a whole organisation with headquarters inside a space training facility? And for what?*]

Balbooza: [*And how?*]

Gee: [*Balbooza, can you see what the sign next to that huge dome says?*]

Balbooza: [*It says...* Star Wars Launch Bay.]

Gee: [*Avengers, astro blasters, space rockets, launch bay, star wars... I don't like the sound of any of it. And it's all labelled with this strange mutant mouse creature Zorn's host body had a tattoo of. Zorn must have been on to them but lost contact before he could report to the mothership. Good thing that you and I could track him here.*]

Balbooza: [*You really think that humans are preparing an invasion? But what's their motive?*]

Gee: [*Can you read those two signs in front of the launch bay?*]

Balbooza: [*"Galactic Grill" and "Alien Pizza Planet".*]

Gee: [*Oh no.*]

Chapter 8

Human Culture and Art

A human culture is a set of values and behaviours that deviate from common sense in a coherent way. While being utterly unreasonable is one of the most defining human traits, being unreasonable in a completely random manner may quickly compromise you as an alien – or worse: earn you the reputation of a human who doesn't quite fit in. Fitting in is one of the primary ethics of human tribalism. Succeeding with it means learning to be unreasonable in the exact same manner as the tribe you are infiltrating.

In the past, human tribes were neatly organised around specific territorial areas and the tribesmen would usually kill off anyone within their area who did not fit in. This made infiltration a very simple matter of doing one piece of homework: learning to behave like the sort of idiot that normally survives in your area of operation.

This convenient practice of killing off everyone you don't understand has gradually been abandoned in favour of the practice of pretending to like differences. As a consequence, knowing which manner of stupidity to adhere to has become increasingly difficult. Humans of different cultures can now co-exist within the same habitation unit and be evenly spread across the area (although they usually aren't because they still secretly hate each other and prefer to stay off each other's porch). In most civilisations, allowing specimens of different cultures to co-inhabit the same area ultimately leads to all coexisting cultures merging into one that makes the most sense.

Humans do not work that way.

They prefer to deviate from reason in unison with only those with whom they share a certain set of qualities and traits, all of which are remarkably unrelated to their mental capabilities.

You may already be familiar with the term "culture" as a clever way of cultivating microorganisms for the purpose of fermentation. Unlike such microorganisms, to whom being cultured is a form of exploitation by larger life forms unable to achieve pure happiness without the aid of intoxicating substances, humans consider being cultured quite prestigious.

The degree to which a human is cultured is usually measured as the degree to which the human is able to appreciate certain products of fermentation produced by aforementioned cultured microorganisms, but also a variety of extremely dubious phenomena that have so little in common apart from being unequivocally useless that humans couldn't find a better term for them than simply "art". The word, we believe, stems from the old human tongue for "things yond simply art" – *things that simply are.*

Understanding art can get you a long way in human society. It is also completely and utterly impossible. What is possible, however, is to pretend to understand art, which is what all supposedly cultured humans spend a great deal of their social interaction time doing. In this chapter, we will look at some of the most common art forms and how you can fake understanding them.

~

The Concept of Identity

Unlike other sentient species, humans do not consider the mere acknowledgement of their own existence to be a sufficient degree of sentience. The strict limits of their mental capacity leave them with a strong urge to categorise themselves and all the surrounding specimens according to a seemingly endless variety of parameters. It can be such parameters as the colour of the human's sparse patches of fur, the types of fuel they consciously refuse to absorb, the type of human they entrust to represent their views when in a position of influence, the part of the planet where they were first ejected from one of the least lucrative areas of another human's body – and many more. The combination of values humans assign themselves on such parameters is what the human calls "identity".

The concept of identity can be rather difficult to comprehend for a species that doesn't have one and where all specimens are merely extensions of one collective intellect that continuously grows by the learnings of each specimen and doesn't die when each specimen dies. Humans do apply a similar hive mind concept in their rudimentary cross-device cloud data storage technology, self-driving ground vehicles and AI chat bots. However, in their physical life they are sealed containers of mostly useless knowledge and a set of bodily anomalies that together constitute their identity.

Although it seems to have little practical use, most humans consider identity to be extremely important and use every given opportunity to manifest theirs to others by means of the way they look, communicate and conduct themselves. It is therefore of paramount importance that you learn how to fabricate and manifest your identity. For that, you will need to learn the main human identity building parameters.

Identity by Proximity to Death

One of the most inconsistent human identity-shaping parameters is age. It is something often used as a measure of a human's development, but can be better described as an approximation of the amount of harm a human is yet capable of inflicting upon the world before vacating it.

The influence of this parameter on the human's identity is constantly changing. As humans are unable to directly pass on their knowledge to their offspring, all of them are born knowing absolutely nothing. Newborn humans are so stupid they cannot even tell the difference between another human and a toilet seat. All knowledge needs to be acquired from a clean slate, which unfortunately means that it will not amount to very much before the human naturally dies. Still, with every year of life the average human grows slightly wiser.

It usually takes a newly produced human a couple of years to learn the benefits of depositing the products of their metabolism in dedicated containers instead of decorating their surroundings with them. After one tenth of a lifetime most humans begin to realise that their planet does not revolve around them. At about one quarter of a lifetime most of them stop using clenched extremities on their frontal appendages as means of diplomatic negotiation. About halfway in they usually realise that they are mortal and begin to adapt their ambitions and plans to the time they have left – only to realise at three quarters in that their plans are all wrong and that their ambitions are entirely incompatible with their capabilities.

You can usually tell how far a human has advanced

in their age by their appearance. Developed humans are usually larger and less mobile than less developed ones. They communicate in a manner that adequately adheres to the rules of human language and social codes. Their hair is more equally spread across their whole body surface compared to younger ones, whose hair is typically concentrated to the head. Their noses are slightly larger and the skin on their faces is not as tightly attached to the skull as it is on undeveloped humans, which makes it significantly easier to remove.

Humans exhibiting these characteristics are the most lucrative abduction targets thanks to their vastly superior knowledge deposits compared to young humans (not that their knowledge has ever been of any practical use other than to cure insomnia through endless recollections of completely unintriguing events). A general rule of thumb at the Galactic Abductee Exchange is that a human's price doubles with every additional decade of life. A common semi-legal price inflating practice among the more opportunistic abductee traders is to stretch the facial skin of their abductees for several days before introducing them to the market in order to produce a more aged look.

Oddly, this valuation model does not seem to resonate at all with the way humans assess their own appearance. For reasons difficult to comprehend, humans are tremendously depressed by the prospect of ageing and prefer to be perceived as less aged than they actually are. They conceal their age data from others, paint their faces with chemicals to mask the looseness of their skin, deliberately distort words in a manner that younger humans would and keep their graduation photo as their permanent social media avatar.

We haven't yet been able to explain this counter-intuitive human fascination with youth. It could have something to do with the fact that humans are mortal and noticeably unamused by the prospect of dying. However, their propensity to annually celebrate the milestone of getting one year closer to death speaks against this hypothesis.

One thing is certain: knowledge is clearly not a primary virtue of this species. You will thus not win any additional social points by going undercover as a highly aged human. Instead, doing so will bring some additional complexity to the way you must conduct yourself.

If the intended age of your human host body is less than twenty percent away from the average human life expectancy, you will have to decrease your movement pace by at least half compared to the already excruciatingly slow human average. You will also need to act as if every fast moving object or loud noise is a threat to your life. Young humans are often puzzled by how scared aged humans are of accidental death, given how little difference a premature death would make in terms of their likely life expectancy. They fail to realise that what aged humans really fear isn't death, but the additional movement pace decrease they would have to live with in case they happen to suffer an accident that fails to kill them.

When undercover as an aged human, you should also apply a similar pace decrease to any outbound communication. You will likely find this part particularly difficult, as you may need to spend ten minutes or more conveying a message that would have taken four milliseconds to broadcast by even the most primitive form of telepathy. To make matters worse, you will need to repeat every piece of your outbound communication at least once an hour for as long as it remains at least remotely relevant.

Overall, you will have to limit your communication to a set number of narratives, which you must repeat an infinite number of times at every given opportunity to humans who have heard them before. Inbound communication will have to be severely restricted. Even when receiving valuable information you must act as if your receptors are dysfunctional and continue repeating your own broadcast as if the recipient's receptors are dysfunctional too. This will ultimately inspire any sane human to find an excuse to free themselves from your company, which you will likely find to be a great relief.

Be careful when choosing your broadcast subjects. Any subject that might be relevant to a young human or exhibiting knowledge about anything a young human might find relevant will be considered highly suspicious. Should you touch upon any such subject, make sure to do so in a strictly condescending manner, comparing it to some prehistoric practice that will not seem the least advantageous to your audience, but making it sound as if it were. When called out on such contradictions, simply remind the audience of their age inferiority and assure them that the gobbledygook you just told them will make perfect sense when they have aged enough. By that time they will not have the mental capacity to recall the promise.

One advantage of going undercover as an aged human is that they are a lot more predictable than young ones, which means that you will only need to memorise a limited number of routes, activities, meal recipes and stories to annoy younger humans with. You can actually achieve a really convincing impression of an aged human simply by sitting perfectly still for several hours and staring at a wall-mounted electronic screen, where another human gets excited by pulling out spherical objects out from a transparent container and joyfully exclaiming the numbers inscribed on them, as if he has just learned how to read.

Aged humans are typically addicted to a stationary broadcasting device known as television. Contrary to what the name suggests, the device cannot visualise telepathic signals, but is merely a re-transmitter of visual recordings made by humans using other forms of primitive two-dimensional recording equipment. The recordings are transmitted simultaneously on multiple channels and cannot be paused, rewound or saved for later. The only way humans can control their reception of the messages is by quickly switching between the different channels, trying to pick up fragments of information broadcasted on each and somehow puzzle them together in their heads. This process is called "channel hopping" (should not be confused with illegal migrant shuttling between France and Britain) and is one of the most popular pastimes among aged humans.

Channel hopping is usually performed by means of an assisting device called a "remote control". Again, do not be tricked by the name or the sophisticated look of the device. Television remote controls look extraordinarily advanced. Unlike most other human-made devices, which typically consist of a flat surface that responds to the touch of human frontal appendages, remote controls look like they have been sent to Earth from another galaxy. Their surface is speckled with dozens of buttons – all marked with hieroglyphs so cryptic even their human owners never learn the meaning of half of them. Aged humans are always sure to refrain from pressing any button they do not understand. Young humans, who are generally unused to handling anything irreversible, would typically press them all, thereby condemning the aged human owner of the television device to days of intensive browsing through a piece of the most unrewarding genre of human literature there is – the television operation manual.

Contrary to the name, apart from channel hopping and occasionally rendering the television set dysfunctional for days, the remote control doesn't really control anything. Our case studies show that pressing many of the buttons produces no effect whatsoever. Infiltrator

Zorn had personally performed one of the studies, where he pressed every single button on a remote control in a variety of scenarios. His 22,346 pages long report concluded that none of the over three million observed objects across the galaxy had moved as a result of pressing any of the buttons. Moreover, the "remote" part is clearly an overstatement. Even the channel hopping doesn't seem to work from any point in the universe except for the small area within a few square metres' proximity of the television screen.

If you are a beginner infiltrator, it is highly recommended that you choose a young human host body. Doing so has several advantages. Young human bodies are more flexible, heal faster and are harder to break. The trading value of a young human on the galactic abductee market is very low, so it will not be much of a loss if you do succeed in breaking it.

Most importantly, the fact that young humans are expected to be stupid gives you a lot of manoeuvring space. The lower the age, the more human social codes you may violate without being compromised.

If you have been severely neglecting your curriculum, your safest option is to go undercover as a toddler. A toddler is a very freshly produced human capable of moving about the planet's surface in a semi-rational manner, but otherwise entirely oblivious to anything beyond its immediate proximity and completely socially incompetent. Being a toddler makes your range of socially acceptable conduct infinitely wide. There is very little you can do while undercover as a toddler that will create any risk of being perceived as an alien. Essentially, almost any behaviour is acceptable. There are only two things you cannot do: using the full human vocabulary and being reasonable.

The vocabulary of a toddler is limited to an average of twenty words, of which three should be used about thirty times more often than the rest of them. One of these is "muh-muh" and refers to the human who believes that she brought you into the world. The second one you may select yourself from the whole range of the aforementioned human's vocabulary. The most common choice is "No". The third one you may make up yourself.

There is no way you will be able to make any sensible conversation with only twenty words, so it doesn't quite matter which ones you choose. Infiltrator Zorn's experiments indicate that surrounding humans best respond to words that describe objects and phenomena that commonly surround a toddler. Strangely, they do not respond well to words that are most relevant to humanity, such as "oxygen", "fuel", "temperature", "overpopulation" or "evacuation".

Limiting your vocabulary to twenty words doesn't mean that all your communication must be confined to these twenty words. There are various other sounds and gestures you may employ to communicate with humans. Just make sure to never be reasonable when doing so. When emitting a sound, make sure it is dispro-portionally loud when delivered to a human in your close proximity. Never focus your attention on anything for more than three seconds, laugh at things that aren't even remotely funny and cry at random.

When crying, make sure that the whole neighbourhood is well aware of you crying. Use the full potential of your vocal chords. Overall, making any movements or sounds at any amplitude and at any time will be perceived as perfectly normal by the surrounding humans. You may not feel the need to make use of this possibility, but please be encouraged to do so. A human toddler that spends more than five minutes without annoying anyone is a potential suspect.

A word of warning: unlike gender, humans do not view age as a subjective notion. An old human who identifies as young is not allowed to change their age or marry someone who identifies as old but has the physiology of a toddler. Teenagers who dress like pensioners are often harassed by their peers – as are pensioners who dress like teenagers. This means that once you have been assigned your host body, you must act in accordance with its age, regardless of how you feel inside. Humans are cruel, but enduring their cruelty is part of your job.

Identity by Gender

Gender is the human idea that manners, appearance and views should be determined by a human's own interpretation of their sex. As explained in a previous chapter, sex is the role a human is designed to play when coupling to produce new humans. In spite of the impression one may get from the multitude of educational videos widely available on human electronic data networks when searching for the term "sex", the human reproduction process really only requires two roles. Neither does it require any of the additional instrumentation you may often see in these instruction videos.

Thus, just like all other terrestrial creatures with the exception of the Auanema worm, humans only have two sexes: female and male. The latter is clearly a short form of the prior, which directly contradicts the actual statistical size difference between the two.

The human sexes are usually easy to tell apart. The most common human interpretation of having at least one testicle is that one is a male, although many females identify males not by testicles but rather by their level of recklessness in the face of danger. A testicle is a fragile organ, critical to human procreation and extremely vulnerable to melee attacks, that the designers of the human body have deliberately placed on the outside of the body – presumably in order to provide the physically inferior human females with a certain escape method when cornered by malevolent males.

With all this said, human interpretations of their sex may vary greatly, constituting an almost infinite number of genders, of which humans have so far only discovered a small fraction. Unlike a human's sex, a human's gender has no practical purpose other than possibly providing an indication of how complicated an attempt to produce offspring with the human in question might be if attempted. Humans do, however, find gender extremely important to their identity. So much, in fact, that a lot of the externally observable artificial attributes of a human – such as apparel, vocabulary, body language and beverage preference – are clearly gendered.

If at this point you feel like giving up your infiltration training at the prospect of having to learn how to accurately determine the gendering of every piece of cloth or drink according to eighty-one known human gender identities – don't panic. Zorn's grand study of the section division in over four million human clothing stores clearly indicates that humans only take three genders seriously: women, men and children. How the latter could be considered a gender has been a matter of some debate. Zorn's conclusion based on the sections in clothing stores is that all human children must have the same gender until they properly mature.

In terms of influence and power, one gender clearly stands out among the rest, and that is the woman (the gender most closely corresponding to the biological programming of the female sex). Most decisions in human societies are either made by or under direct influence of women – except for the really poor ones, which are usually made by men (a gender constructed entirely around the male sex and much preoccupied with it) independently as an attempt to assert their illusion of authority. This illusion is rather intricately and cunningly upheld by women. They usually allow men, who are male by sex and therefore biologically inferior in their risk assessment capabilities, to assume the most exposed positions of power. Men in such extremely vulnerable positions are then easily influenced in their decisions by women who, as men eventually fail miserably, may conveniently use their failures as leverage in the discourse about gender power disparity, thereby effectively elevating their chances of assuming the positions of power which should be reasonably desirable to any reasonable being.

Identity by Pride and Shame

One rather remarkable trait which humans regard as strongly identity defining is the ability to be sexually attracted to an individual, with whom coupling does not enable further spread of one's genome. Although multiple highly cherished human societal phenomena, such as male fashion and the Eurovision Song Contest, wouldn't have existed if not for this ability, many of those who possess it tend to conceal it so well that they sometimes even manage to trick themselves into believing that they don't have it. Although any other galactic civilisation would applaud any skill that decreases the risk of more humans being produced, our brain scan research on human subjects possessing this ability reveals that such stealthy behaviour is somehow fuelled by deep shame.

We aren't sure about the source of this shame, but

our observations show that once every time Earth makes a full circle around its star, this shame tends to suddenly reverse into a feeling of great pride. At that point the aforementioned humans suddenly put on artificial trusses of long fur onto their heads, dress up in a manner very rarely seen on this planet and march out into the streets, trotting them for many hours and making great amounts of noise. This very dubious expression of pride tends to greatly enrage certain bald humans, who presumably feel taunted by all the superfluous head fur and often confront the proud trotters, insisting that the latter should cease being proud and go back to being ashamed.

Although humans with this sexual preference are not able to procreate together with their objects of attraction, it doesn't mean that aren't trying to. When going undercover as this sort of human, be prepared for everything you have ever learned about human mating habits to be challenged. You can effectively use this to your advantage. Zorn's chronicles indicate that human abductees from this particular stratum tend to be a lot more open-minded about intrusive research than other humans if you manage to present it as something truly fabulous.

Identity by Location

In which area of Earth's dry surface a human makes first contact with the planet's atmosphere appears to be strongly defining to the human's identity. Although humans are rarely given a choice on where exactly to escape their initial nine-month-long confinement inside another human's body, the location always marks the human with a social label which is almost impossible to remove. The label is known as "nationality" and is supposed to create affinity with other humans who escaped their cocoon host bodies in the same area – regardless how little they actually have in common.

Unlike sexual orientation, nationality is something humans tend to be tremendously proud of all year around. You will notice that few things entertain a human more than talking endlessly about the distinguishing features of language, fuel combinations, history and shared personality disorders of the nationality they believe themselves to belong to – especially if the nationality of the speaking human does not correlate with the country the human is currently in. This pride does not seem to in any way correlate with the general popularity of the human's nationality or its defining features among other humans. The most despised nationalities on Earth evoke equally strong pride among their representatives as the most popular ones.

Throughout its horrifically bloody history of violent tribalism, there have been very few occasions when significant numbers of humans have felt even remotely ashamed of their nationality, regardless of how many monstrous atrocities, at which scale, and at however high levels of representation their countrymen have committed. Even those enlightened humans who are perfectly aware of their nationality's low standing in the world, and who genuinely regret their affiliation with it, tend to side with their despicable nation in conflicts even against the most respected and morally righteous nations – even when their own nation was at fault for the conflict. It is a strange defining characteristic of humans to be prepared to die for something they didn't choose.

A very simple way of manifesting your nationality is by using a flag. Flags are mostly rectangular rags with colour patterns which humans like to string onto a staff and stick into things they lay claims on, thereby severely overcomplicating a task which dogs easily solve without any additional equipment. (Colourful rectangular rags *without* a staff are called "beach towels" and are commonly used by humans for the exact same purpose.) Placing a flag in your proximity will clearly state your affiliation with a certain nation. Although an average human is only able to recognise fifteen out of the over two hundred human national flags, the chance of recognition is considerably higher than the chance of a human recognising the smell of their countrymen's urine.

You can effectively use nationality as a cover for your inadequate human culture training by pretending to have a nationality that is foreign to the country you are infiltrating. Your most certain strategy would be to present yourself with a nationality very few have heard anything about and which is hard to even pronounce in most human languages, like the Kyrgyz (not to be confused with the quadruped fungus civilisation Kyrghyz inhabiting planet Gxhrymzykyhr in the 44 Boötis System). Should you, by sheer bad luck, happen to end up in the company of a real Kyrgyz while impersonating one, pretend that you have a speech defect that makes "Australian" sound like "Kyrgyz" and move away slowly while making unintelligible sounds.

Identity by Race

Although all humans look more or less the same to any extraterrestrial being and are more or less indistinguishable from other apes, among themselves they like to classify each other by race. The primary practical benefit of doing so is the number of adjectives it saves you when trying to verbally describe the appearance of a human who isn't present. In some parts of the planet it may also grant you additional education and career boosting privileges provided that you have selected a human body suite of any race but one.

If you are a beginner infiltrator, however, you will do best to avoid these parts for your first mission. The reason for that is that the identity-building effect of race tends to get disturbingly pronounced in places where humans of multiple races coexist.

The vast majority of human settlements are monoethnic. When infiltrating them, you will simply need to make sure that your human costume is of the same race as the rest of the population in the area. Humans in such areas don't ponder much about race because they are all of the same one and it therefore has little to no impact on their identity, demeanour and speech.

The few areas that are multi-ethnic, however, are not for beginners. In these areas you will need to make significant adjustments to the way you dress, speak and what kinds of noise you deliberately expose yourself to, depending on the race of your human costume.

Worst of all, apart from the risk of being compromised, there is also a penalty for behaving in a manner which locals associate with humans of a different race than the one you have chosen. Humans call such conduct either "cultural appropriation" or "cultural exchange", depending on the race of the perpetrator. It may not sound like it has anything to do with race, but since humans are an extremely racist species, many of them find it appropriate for a human's race to define that human's culture, and they find it inappropriate for a human of a different race to share that culture.

This is just one method by which humans in racially diverse areas have masterfully succeeded in preserving a high level of racial and cultural segregation for many centuries, with racially biased cultural differences reproducing themselves generation after generation. Another effective method for racial segregation they have used is colonial slavery, but this one is no longer available to most humans.

～

Music and Dancing

Of all the various parameters that comprise a human's identity, few have a greater impact on a human's appearance and conduct than the kind of sounds a human likes. You will notice that apart from the natural sounds emitted by the human body or produced through its collision with other objects, humans have a habit of artificially producing sounds that follow certain deliberate patterns. To an alien all such sound patterns would seem equally nauseating, but to a human, the emotional reaction to different human-made sounds can vary from ecstatic bliss to suicidal depression.

It can be quite astounding how much trouble a human can be prepared to go through only to produce a certain sound pattern – something they often do in collaboration with other humans and by means of a whole arsenal of special tools. The process may at times appear so sophisticated it could even leave you with the false impression that the humans are actually doing something useful. They call the product of this activity "music".

The distinction between music and other human-made sounds is not entirely clear, but you can usually tell the difference by the way other humans react to the sounds. If you notice them rocking their bodies or beating the top of their thighs or close-by surfaces with their frontal limbs, then it's probably music. If they cap their ears with their limbs and wince in terror and disgust – it can still be music, only of a kind that does not fit well with their identity.

This latter case is the reason why it is so crucial for every alien infiltrator to identify which kind of music is appreciated within the stratum of humans among which you are stationed and how to move your body when it is played. Failing at this is very likely to get you compromised and video recordings of you moving inaccurately to music to be spread across human social media as a warning for other humans to be more vigilant. Below follow descriptions of some of the most prominent and identity shaping music types – each with an instruction on how to behave when you hear them.

Electronic Dance Music

This type of music often appears in places that are overcrowded with humans. It is easily recognised by a loud pounding sound hammering mercilessly at your eardrums at short even intervals, occasionally accompanied by other less prominent noises, such as various nagging and wailing produced by means of human vocal cords and endlessly repeating a brief message of dubious purpose.

The source of the sound can usually be tracked to a human in the room wearing large defective earmuffs that constantly need to be upheld by one limb. This human possesses a device with multiple buttons and toggles, one of which has the ability to stop all this sonic pollution. It usually takes the human four to six hours to find that toggle. Until then the human will typically stand idly with a concerned look on their face while toying with various other buttons and toggles that have absolutely no impact on the pre-recorded wall of sound the surrounding human crowd is exposed to.

If you are caught up in a context like this, you will blend in best by keeping both of your back appendages firmly on the planet surface while slightly bending your knees and performing a variety of movements with your frontal appendages. More or less any movements will qualify as normal in this situation, but the most common one would be to contract your fingers in a fist and pretend to repeatedly hit an invisible target slightly above your head while turning your face down towards the planet surface and shutting your eyelids, as if to prevent any splinter from the invisible object you are attempting to break from damaging your eyes.

Hip Hop Music

This genre is sometimes difficult to distinguish from a plain human conversation where one human is angrily telling off and threatening another human. The difference can be revealed by the accompanying beating sound which, oddly, tends to begin before the threats. Unlike the typical sound of an assault, a hip hop track begins with a human (sometimes several) expressing overstated agreement by means of affirmative phrases and exclamations, before any statement has been made to which these affirmations may logically refer. The beating sound that usually accompanies such expressions of agreement may appear misplaced at first, but usually both the tone and the message of the human gets a lot less agreeable as the sound track progresses. The message is usually directed at someone the human is displeased with.

Because confirmation appears to be an important part of hip hop music, the expected manner of conduct when hearing it is to nod your head in agreement. Try not to overdo it by nodding it too fast. Many humans who enjoy hip hop music do not appreciate humans who are overly enthusiastic. Use the beating sound as a sonic marker for each nod.

Sometimes the situation may call for more convincing movements – especially when you find yourself surrounded by heavily armed humans who happen to be strongly fond of hip hop music. Your safest way of adopting a fitting movement pattern for such occasions is to study other terrestrial primates – especially males competing for deposits of fresh fruit or for the attention of females of the same primate species.

To add some additional human flavour to your movements, try thrusting the extremities of your front appendages forward as if trying to speed-dry your recently painted fingernails by creating artificial air waves while holding a microchip between the tips of two or three fingers on each hand. This will look more convincing if you wear clothes made for extremely obese humans and relax all your facial muscles to a point where you start looking slightly sedated.

Rock Music

This genre of music is largely derived from a tool called "guitar", which humans have developed a habit of subjecting to an excessive amount of electric current. This makes the guitar squeak like a wounded tyrannosaurus when touched, forcing the human to stretch their vocal cords to the limit of their ability in order for any message to break through the artificial wall of deafening noise.

Contrary to what the name suggests, you will not necessarily be expected to rock when rock music is played. You will, however, be expected to express even more convincing agreement than when hearing hip hop music. You will need to nod your head even more intensively, sometimes at four times the pace compared to hip hop, and in a much longer trajectory. Unlike with hip hop, the clothes you should wear must barely fit your body. Ideally, they should be made of shaven animal skin and painted black.

To blend in even better, it is highly recommended to stretch out one of your frontal limbs in a 45 degrees upwards angle with three fingers contracted together and two pointing in the same direction as the limb.

Depending on which specific fingers you point with and which ones you hold together, the effect may be very different, so please make sure to use the correct ones. You will know that you have chosen suitable fingers to point with if the distance between them approximately equals the distance between an adult human's eyes. (For this reason, always make sure that you stand facing the same direction as the surrounding humans when performing this movement.)

This exercise may be tiresome, but you must never succumb to the temptation to unfold your hand and point all five of your fingers in the same direction while your limb is in this position. There are sub-genres of rock music where this would be appropriate, but in most cases you will attract undesired attention.

Pop Music

Music that almost entirely lacks the ability to make any human sick with disgust or fall asleep is called "pop". It usually consists of human voices lamenting practical difficulties around mating in a curiously self-confident and upbeat manner, supported by various artificial noises and beating sounds. These lamentations are usually addressed to some unnamed baby.

Humans who deliver these messages typically wear a lot less clothing than average humans and a lot more makeup. They tend to move their bodies in rather unnatural ways and slowly shake their heads in disagreement as they pronounce their message, regardless of its content.

You aren't really expected to do anything or wear anything particular when pop music is played, because pop music is a kind of music that is extremely difficult for humans to build their identity around. What you should avoid doing is discuss this music with humans, because humans who listen to pop music never really listen to it and rarely ever care what it is about. Trying to be intellectual about it may raise their suspicion about the authenticity of your humanity.

If sitting still and ignoring these foul sounds is simply too much of an effort for you, you may try nodding your head in moderate agreement or, if your host body is female, rocking the rear part of the body sideways at a pace that matches the intervals between the loudest beating sounds. If your host body is male, just keep your feet firmly attached to the ground and move the rest of your body as if you were a slightly sedated baboon. Such behaviour usually transcends into something humans call "dancing".

Dancing

As you can see, nearly all music may, at times, produce the necessity for you to perform various bodily movements if you are to fully live up to the expectations of natural human behaviour. Humans moving semi-synchronously to artificially synthesised sound is called "dancing". Originally a mating ritual, this peculiar behaviour has almost entirely lost its initial purpose to a point where it most frequently aids misguided white males in perpetuating their celibacy.

It is quite hard to explain dancing to a non-terrestrial being. The wide variety of its manifestations and patterns makes it almost impossible to establish an accurate movement pattern in each given context, which is why it is strongly recommended to simply mimic the movements of the surrounding humans. This is usually easy enough as long as you can distinguish who is dancing and who is simply moving about.

You can usually tell dancing from other human body movements by the apparent lack of purpose in the movements. However, mind that there are certain human health conditions that may bring about involuntary purposeless body movements. For your information, a dance is not likely to be accompanied by excessive foaming salivation.

Another important insight is that dancing seldom involves heavy non-human objects. If you see a human making unnatural and seemingly purposeless movements that involve lifting up a heavy object with observably great effort – make sure that the object is not a human by either asking it, poking it on the sides to elicit laughter or by offering it a discount coupon. If the object does not respond, then the object is either a dead human – or the human lifting it is not actually dancing, but rather building additional muscle. If the object responds, then what you are seeing is an example of what humans call "ballroom dancing", where the female part of the couple is just extremely obese and the lifting male is unusually strong.

Ballroom dancing is a type of dance humans use as an excuse for touching each other's bodies without being suspected of sexual harassment. Normally, standing very close to another human, especially one of another sex, is considered rude and intrusive. Holding the human by both hands and looking them straight in the eye while doing so is considered even more inappropriate, especially if the human is socially or legally engaged with another human. Being caught by the human's spouse while doing this is certain to bring about an unpleasant conversation at the least – or a painful and disgraceful death at the worst, depending on who the spouse is. Ballroom dancing, however, removes this constraint completely.

If you are operating a male body, you may walk up to a married human couple and ask the male whether you may dance with his wife. If the male agrees, which they most often do, then you may do all the above, squeeze the female against your body, touch her and stare right into her eyes right in front of her spouse without any risk of retribution.

Please mind that not all body contact is considered acceptable when ballroom dancing. Infiltrator Zorn's multiple dancefloor experiments have shown that inserting objects into another human's body while dancing with them is seldom well received by any involved party. You are therefore advised to abstain from conducting research on human subjects when on the dancefloor. With that said, ballroom dancing is a splendid opportunity for abduction, as it appears to make it highly desirable for humans who have presently been engaged in a dance with you to follow you to places which humans otherwise seldom agree to accompany strangers to.

Do not be confused by the absence of balls in the room where you are expected to engage in ballroom dancing. As counter-intuitive as it may sound, rooms with a surplus of balls are usually the ones least fit for the purpose – at least according to infiltrator Zorn's report, detailing the circumstances around him being forcibly removed from a ball pool in a shopping mall, where he had made some futile attempts at tango with the surrounding human infants. The report stated that the infants exhibited a very poor sense of rhythm and seemed increasingly distraught by their own failure. Throwing Zorn's dead clown into the ball pool showed to be of little use in raising their spirits.

One type of dancing that has ventured off particularly far from its original purpose is ballet. Essentially, ballet is an act where heavily undernourished humans try to impress wealthy elders by pretending to be immune to gravity. Thanks to the extremely light weight of their starved bodies, ballet dancers are able to bounce about the stage by elegantly surfing on bursts of air emitted by the brass instruments in the orchestra pit. The gliding is often supported by a light circular fan around the human's waist, which acts both as a sail and a stabiliser capable of keeping the dancer erect when occasionally fainting due to low blood sugar levels.

~

Visual Art

Humans are widely known for their propensity to transform the extremely limited natural resources of their planet into artificial products that benefit their needs but are utterly useless to other life forms. Occasionally, they manage to transform Earth's resources into products that are entirely useless to humans too. Such products are called "pieces of art". We still haven't managed to decipher exactly what art is, but the general difference between a piece of art and a piece of any other entirely useless substance seems to reside in the fact that art is something humans are occasionally prepared to pay for.

One common type of art that humans sometimes are prepared to pay quite a lot for are two-dimensional images of various more or less recognisable objects, which humans like to attach to the inner walls of their habitat, facing inwards. For many centuries the primary motive of such images were depictions of various sections of Earth's surface, which led many of us to believe that the purpose of this art form was to compensate for the shortage of windows.

Another common motive of such images – faces and bodies of other, sometimes completely unfamiliar humans, was believed to be meant to compensate for the owner's lack of social interaction. It wasn't until Zorn's infiltration mission in the early 20th century Spain, where he went undercover as a painter named Pablo Picasso, that we learned of the true purpose of visual art. Zorn went undercover as an artist because according to our statistics, humans with artistic talent are extremely unlikely to be discovered. In order to further decrease his chances of being discovered, Zorn deliberately made his watercolour depictions of humans extremely poor – sometimes to the point of non-recognisability. Oddly, however hard he tried to ruin his work, he kept receiving more and more attention – and more and more orders, hardly leaving him any time to commit to any serious intelligence work.

It was when his most hideous depiction of some human females he had abducted (and accidentally dismembered) in the very home-planet-like state of Algiers hit his bidding record that Zorn finally concluded what it was that humans liked so much about visual art. It isn't the perceived beauty or the accuracy of depiction that pleases the human eye. It is the symbolism of all the careless destruction embedded in the work that really appeals to humans – the most destructive and careless creature known to science.

Exploiting limited planetary oil resources to produce paint, chopping down trees to make a palette, shaving ponies to produce brushes, utilising good cotton to make a canvas and then wasting a whole day on ruining the image of a moderately attractive woman by applying it to the canvas, thereby rendering both the canvas, the brushes and the woman entirely useless for any further exploitation – that is what constitutes the value of human art. Whenever humans feel that they haven't been destructive or wasteful enough, they may look at their wall art and immediately feel better about themselves.

The above conclusion immediately solved the long living puzzle of why humans are prepared to pay fortunes for vaguely accurate depictions of reality that is otherwise perfectly observable outside the human habitat and can be easily and far more accurately depicted by means of the high resolution cameras all humans carry with them at all times. However beautiful the depiction, it will not be worth much if no suffering and destruction was involved in producing it. A photograph is only truly valuable if the photographer has spent immense amounts of money on their camera equipment, countless hours on finding the right spot and calibrating the equipment only to have to start over again and again due to worsened weather conditions, had to track the object of depiction through extremely hostile terrain at the peril of death and preferably died as a consequence of retribution right after passing the photograph to the press.

For reasons laid out above, you would be wise not to go undercover as a visual artist. However, if you want to gain the trust of the most influential humans on Earth, you should be prepared to talk about art a lot more than it deserves. When doing so, make sure to never give a hint of what you really think of art and its uselessness.

You will blend in best if you attempt to always elevate the skill of the artist when pretending to appreciate a piece of art. Pretend to see meaning in every random stroke and every accidental blot the artist has attempted to smudge over and re-purpose into something artistic. If the painter failed in maintaining natural symmetry when attempting to add perspective at an odd angle – try to compliment the artist for challenging reality by enriching space with a faint touch of a fourth dimension. If the humans in the painting exhibit severe deviations from the basic human anatomy – praise the artist's bold defiance of conventional canons of beauty. If the painting looks like it could have been painted by a toddler – celebrate the artist for calling out the yoke of perfection and encouraging the spectators to seek real beauty in the cradle of perfect simplicity. If the painting looks like it has been vomited onto the canvas by a Saturnian nitrogen-blooded scavenger eel – pretend to admire the artist's brilliant ability to set colour to the very point where loneliness and anxiety briefly merge into hope, only to transcend into agony and disgust a moment later.

SUBHUMAN CODES AND DIFFERENCES

To humans, knowledge almost always comes second after habit. Habit is a common terrestrial mechanism that puts every new learned behaviour on autopilot that has no "off" button. New superior knowledge isn't capable of stopping the inertia of a habitual behaviour or opinion.

In order to improve, a human needs to manually deconstruct the habit while it is active and force the new behaviour into its place, thereby risking the stability of one's whole mental system of coordinates. Humans rarely make this effort willingly only for the sake of personal improvement. Therefore, they tend to forever stick with most behaviours, values and codes they have learned early in life, however obsolete and irrational these may be. This stickiness is what constitutes the fabric of human culture, and because most of the sticky stuff is learned in the geographic context of a human's upbringing, you will find different human cultures in different areas of the planet.

Of course, some cultural elements are universally human. Regardless of where they are raised, all humans will become hostile when you deprive them of their property, mate with their spouse or position your slowly moving vehicle in front of theirs on a single-lane road. All humans will become friendly if you can make them believe that they may receive something valuable from you and they will only nail you to a piece of wood when they are tremendously displeased with you.

If your infiltration mission requires you to travel to multiple areas of Earth, you would benefit from learning which human cultural codes vary by location and which are universal. Which one is rarely possible to guess. For instance, the desire to deliberately intoxicate oneself with noxious liquids and substances is universal across the whole human population, but the specific choice of such liquids and substances depends very much on the human's culture. The number of kisses required to properly greet another human depends on the human's culture, while the number of attempts required to plug in a USB cable is consistently three all over the world.

Some human cultures will require quite significant adaptation. For example, if you are deployed inside the country called the United States, you will blend in best by ensuring that the size of any property or equipment you are wielding is at least thirty percent greater than anywhere else on Earth. This includes the size of your body wrapping, the size of your meals and the size of the vehicle you will need to employ to get about, regardless of terrain.

In order to avoid American humans ever doubting that you are one of them, it is advised that you place a United States flag visibly next to your supposed habitat, inside your vehicle and preferably on some of your clothes. The further away from the large human cities you get, the more necessary this becomes, as you will notice by the increasing density of flags the further away you move from urban areas. You must also pretend to be extremely proud to call yourself American and to believe that the United States is the best country in the world, while at the same time pretending to never have been to any other human country and seeming unaware of most human countries even existing.

The latter is a common manifestation of something humans call "patriotism" – a universally human form of self-deception that invigorates an individual with a strong sense of loyalty towards a certain patch of planetary surface where the human was brought into existence – regardless of how awful it is (both the patch and the existence).

Simulating patriotism is a hard act to pull off, but mastering it will help you establish closer bonds with humans in most other human countries as well. However, according to Zorn's experiments, simulating patriotism towards the United States works best when you are actually in the United States. Doing it in other countries may produce mixed reactions, with the occasional side effect of shoes being thrown at ambassadors, perfectly new flags being burned and aircraft crashing into skyscrapers.

Many of our infiltrators have wished that they had been warned in advance about some of the specific peculiarities of certain human cultures that would have made their missions a lot less traumatising. For instance, when deployed in England, make sure to never deliver any negative information as it is. Doing so is considered by humans of England to be preposterously rude. Instead, you should embed any such information in a disproportionately large amount of apologies, even if the necessity to convey this information is not your fault but theirs. For example, when needing to inform a human that their vehicle needs to be removed from a parking spot for the reason of that spot having been reserved for and pre-paid by you, you must phrase it as if that human is a victim of a terrible misfortune caused by you. To appear genuinely English when doing so, try to further enrich any such statement with as many courtesy phrases as you can think of.

Should you, on the other hand, become a victim of a terrible misfortune, such as your vehicle being vandalised and set on fire with you in it by the afore-mentioned human, who may not have taken well to your previous request due to your rookie impoliteness, make sure to downplay the severity of the incident to a level of minor insignificance. If your vehicle is rendered unusable, say it's perfectly fine and was an old piece of rubbish anyway. If your human costume has suffered third-degree full-body burns, dismiss it as a mere scratch and change the subject to something less distressing to your surroundings.

If it's your first time on Earth, we recommend Islamic Sharia societies as your entry point. These societies are very beginner-friendly. They offer one single code of conduct that is very consistently followed and has only two subtypes which are clearly connected to the human's sex. Islamic Sharia societies have only two genders and only one sexual orientation. We are not sure how they do it, but presumably they have developed some elaborate technology that ensures flawlessly binary gendering and sexuality assignment at birth.

Sharia societies have a very simple dress code, which will spare you the trouble of taking the rather advanced human fashion course. The extremely convenient design standard of female apparel will not only spare you the necessity of facial maintenance, but may actually allow you to walk about without your human costume, wearing only the clothes directly on top of your natural body (if you have one).

Best of all, the humans in Sharia societies tend to be extremely helpful in advising you how to behave as a good human and will point out loudly every mistake you make in your conduct. Occasionally they will gather around you and yell the mistake at you, just to make sure that you have clearly received the message. Some may even throw shoes and stones at you in order to get your attention firmly focused on the error. It doesn't quite help us absorb the knowledge, but the fact that humans often use phrases like "That'll teach him!" while applying violence to others, suggests that such methods do work on humans.

~

Zorn search party telepathic intercom transmission excerpt 8

Transmitted two hours, two minutes and eighteen seconds after the second dispatch.

. . .

Balbooza: [*I think I see the target!*]

Gee: [*Zorn?*]

Balbooza: [*No, that mutant creature, Mickey Mouse. It's right there, grabbing human offspring.*]

Gee: [*Indeed... It looks remarkably similar to the tattoo. Frankly, Balbooza, I somehow thought that tattoo was a distorted depiction of a more conventional terrestrial animal. Humans do that a lot. It's called "art". But this one really looks like the freak in the tattoo. What kind of animal do you think it is?*]

Balbooza: [*I've searched the terrestrial fauna database I managed to download at the zoo and got no matches. The closest thing I found is called a* koala, *but the similarities are very remote. It is bipedal, which is something very few terrestrial creatures are, and its eyes are roughly ten times the size of those of the largest known terrestrial mammal. Very unconventional...*]

Gee: [*Check the large fluffy bipedal creatures next to it waving their huge paws. They are grabbing human offspring too. Maybe they are related.*]

Balbooza: [*I did. Nothing. Except for the one in the black coat and sunglasses with a large candy bar in his hand dragging the child he just grabbed towards his vehicle. That one's human. The rest of them seem completely alien to Earth. The closest match I got was a walrus, and we both know by now what a walrus looks like.*]

Gee: [*Not nearly as merry as these furry critters.*]

Balbooza: [*I think that walrus at the zoo liked you. It kept following you around as if it wanted you to stay. Then I guess it got a bit disappointed when you tried to use its tusk to shave me, thereof the sulkiness.*]

Gee: [*Isn't life just full of disappointments... Alright, Balbooza, let's get a closer look at these big furry things.*]

Balbooza: [*What strange creatures! They sound and move a lot like humans, but they all seem to belong to entirely different species. Perhaps they are dogs?*]

Gee: [*Why dogs?*]

Balbooza: [*I read that humans have been deliberately breeding different dog races to make them more different from each other. Apparently, some are now so different that one dog race may look more similar to a different species than to another dog race. They are also said to have embraced much of the human lifestyle – like living indoors, sleeping in beds and eating from bowls at regular times, so maybe that includes walking on two legs, talking, waving frontal appendages at people and grabbing human offspring.*]

Gee: [*Balbooza, I think there are humans inside these creatures.*]

Balbooza: [*You think they eat humans?! Is that why they are grabbing them? What if they eat us? We look very human. You, at least. We must activate the security protocol...*]

Gee: [*I mean there are humans inside these creatures operating them.*]

Balbooza: [*What?! Why would someone operate another creature's body from the inside?*]

Gee: [*Did you seriously just ask me that?*]

Balbooza: [*Oh, right, yes, but we are on a space infiltration mission... Wait, are you saying...*]

Gee: [*We are inside a human space training facility packed with launch pads and rockets ready to embark on some sort of space vengeance war mission and bring home some fresh ingredients for their alien pizza. We find humans disguised as creatures who, as you yourself put it, look entirely alien to Earth. Which part of this do you believe does not fit?*]

Balbooza: [*They are preparing infiltrators!*]

Gee: [*And Zorn was on to them – that's why he must have picked that host body. He wasn't just panicking – he is a cunning schemer, that Zorn. He wanted to infiltrate an infiltration camp.*]

Balbooza: [*Hail Zorn! So which planet do you think they are planning to send these infiltrators to? I cannot recall any inhabited planet in the galaxy with creatures that look like this.*]

Gee: [*There are thousands of inhabited planets in our galaxy crawling with trillions of species. Judging by how diligently you have studied the instruction manual before this mission, I wouldn't presume you have studied all of them, or am I wrong?*]

Balbooza: [*I am more about learning by doing...*]

Gee: [*Never mind. I believe we have found Zorn.*]

Balbooza: [*Really? Where is he then?*]

Gee: [*You are looking at him.*]

Balbooza: [*You are Zorn???*]

Gee: [*No, not me, you imbecile! The human inside*

Mickey Mouse is Zorn. Don't you get it? This is the perfect double infiltration disguise – an alien in a human body dressed up as an alien inside a human space facility. And he gave us the perfect clue to how to find him by exposing the Mickey Mouse tattoo to the person whose trousers he had stolen and put on the chimp, which he knew would be the closest point of infiltration for his search party.]

Balbooza: *[Brilliant! Zorn is a genius!]*

Gee: *[Now let's get him out of here. Remember, he has no transponder, so he cannot receive our telepathic signals. We will have to speak to him as humans. And you are a chimpanzee, so I will have to do the talking.]* Zorn, I'm agent Gee from the mothership. This is agent Balbooza. We came to bring you back. Come with us!

Balbooza: *[I don't think he can hear you, Gee. All these little humans hanging around and grabbing him are too loud.]*

Gee: *[I will try to speak louder.]* ZORN! GREAT ZORN, THE PIONEER INFILTRATOR! WE ARE HERE TO BEAM YOU UP TO THE MOTHERSHIP! *[Balbooza, I don't think I can outshout thirteen human children. We need to remove them.]*

Balbooza: *[Should I liquidise them with my proton blaster?]*

Gee: *[No, there could be collateral. Just pick them off him one by one. They're not that heavy. I'll help.]*

Balbooza: *[On it! The larger humans seem to disapprove of us throwing the small ones off.]*

Gee: [*It doesn't matter. Let's just do it quickly and be off with Zorn.*

Balbooza: [*They sound very upset and threatening.*]

Gee: [*Relax, this will be over in a minute. There, last human removed.*] Zorn, let's go!

Balbooza: [*Why isn't Zorn responding?*]

Gee: [*I don't know. They must have drugged him or something. That would explain all the jumping and grabbing. Grab his hands and lead him to the beaming point.*]

Balbooza: [*Gee, he is not cooperating!*]

Gee: [*Oh, for the love of Space, we have no time for this! They have clearly messed with his head. We'll have to pull him by force.*]

Balbooza: [*Why does he keep protesting and talking about all the crying human offspring?*]

Gee: [*This mission must have been too much for him. Just keep pulling him with us! The pickup point should be inside the building with all those jumping cadavers. Dispatcher, activate the beam!*]

Chapter 9

Human Societies and How to Control Them

The primary purpose of your infiltration mission is to secure the safety of the galaxy by preventing humans from doing to other planets what they do to Earth. Ever since the undoubtedly effective practice of extermination of sentient species has been discontinued by a special decree of the Galactic Council, the only legal way of preventing humans from infesting other planets is by learning to control them.

Fortunately, humans are one of the easiest organisms to control. If you have carefully read the chapter about human belief systems you should know by now that humans regard reality as a matter of choice. This means that it is possible to make humans believe more or less any nonsense – even something that entirely contradicts their immediately observable reality – just by making it appear attractive to them.

Once, in the early 18th century, when struggling to find a good argument for why a human landowner should purchase a defective serf from him at the same price as one with all limbs still attached, infiltrator Zorn (then undercover as a Caribbean slave trader) spontaneously dropped the rather ridiculous remark that all humans are fundamentally equal. What Zorn meant was, of course, that all humans are equally defective anyway in being useful for anything substantially important. However, the remark was overheard by a bystanding Swiss wine merchant named Jean-Jaques Rousseau, who had just finished cleaning up after a very ill-attended wine tasting event.

The latter got so excited by the remark that he dedicated a whole book to the idea. The book was greatly appreciated by the majority of the roughly two hundred individuals in the neighbouring France who could read. The idea was then eagerly retold to the remaining populace, most of whom had never before been indulged with the notion of being equal to anything other than a medium-sized pile of humanium.

Very soon Zorn's clumsy bargaining attempt had turned into a mass belief that led to the establishment of a new societal order across the planet. Even at the present level of scientific development, despite all available statistics on infant mortality, mutations, IQ differences, chronic diseases and household wealth, many humans still believe that all humans are born equal.

Even among those who realise the absurdity of the notion, most would insist that all humans should be treated equally and be granted the same rights. Not even the fact that almost every human who subscribes to this view has a consistent habit of giving humans who share their chromosome structure priority in just about everything appears to be able to shatter this conviction. You should not be surprised to hear the opinion that all humans are equal from a human who on that very same day had uttered the opinion that family always comes first.

~

THE POWER OF MYTH

It is not that humans aren't capable of rational thinking. They are (to an extent). They just choose to apply it selectively when it suits their desires. You will therefore not be able to get very far with this species by appealing to their rationality in matters where the rational truth is less attractive than the irrational belief they currently hold. You will, on the other hand, win their full devotion if you manage to accurately assess their desires and fashion a belief that appeals to them. This has been our primary strategy ever since the incidental insight famously known across the galaxy as the *Valhalla Joke*.

The insight was provided by infiltrator Zorn during his mediaeval infiltration mission as a Viking chieftain. In those early days our core method of keeping the human population at bay was to infiltrate key leadership positions in human societies and use them to maintain a steady level of inter-human conflict. Wars and scuffles would be continuously instigated with neighbouring tribes, ensuring that at least as many humans would be killed as there were born during every time unit. The main challenge with this policy has ever been the base human reluctance to see themselves or their relatives killed.

In his mission report Zorn has documented multiple awkward conversations he had had with the children of warriors who had departed or gone missing, where he was repeatedly questioned about what would happen to their fathers if they were killed. The children reportedly found Zorn's explanations about their fathers' bodies slowly decomposing and being processed through digestive systems of various parasites before re-emerging as scattered piles of manure quite depressing. Emphasising the strong soil fertilisation benefits of worm manure for future crops was only mildly comforting.

Zorn soon noticed that humans seemed generally depressed by the prospect of dying and that the high likelihood of becoming a pile of worm manure had a discouraging effect on the young Vikings' commitment to waging wars on behalf of their chieftain.

Once, annoyed by having to state the obvious once more to yet another young human inquiring about the aftereffects of dying in battle, Zorn allowed himself to respond with a sarcastic joke. He said with a smirk that dying in battle imminently leads to the acquisition of a VIP ticket to a high society nightclub called Valhalla, where the party never stops and where all deceased warriors have free access to an unlimited supply of food and alcoholic beverages.

It had slipped Zorn's mind that the concept of sarcasm hadn't yet been discovered by the humans of the Iron Age. Having found Zorn's answer positively reassuring, the young Viking convinced several of his friends to join the upcoming raid on a neighbouring village on the very next day, during which they were all successfully slaughtered and then cheered all the way to Valhalla by their proud (although slightly envious) mothers. Every human in Zorn's tribe seemed completely convinced that the unlucky raiders were already feasting in Valhalla. Not even the sight of the raiders' mutilated bodies scattered across the blood-stained battlefield could shatter their conviction.

Thus, Zorn's innocent Valhalla joke came to serve as a tide turning insight about the immense power of myth over the human mind.

Myth is a tool more powerful in controlling humanity than the recently invented psionic remote control is in controlling the hive mind of the Mercurian extremophile bacterium civilization of Tuioiuo. It has the power to usher whole human societies in any direction its authors prescribe. Not even the most enlightened humans possessing the greatest intellectual abilities and fully proficient in rational reasoning are entirely immune to its influence. Once properly established in a society, the power of myth is almost impossible to deconstruct, and the few who attempt to do so will be immediately swept away by a violent wave of fanatics and forced to either submit to the myth, withdraw from public sight or perish entirely.

You should therefore always consider myth to be your primary tool – both when coercing individual humans into desired behaviours and when trying to influence society-level events.

This may sound challenging, but it doesn't have to be if you focus your attention on the right things. Most infiltrators spend too much time trying to invent a myth that is plausible and logically consistent. That is entirely unnecessary. As shown by the example of the largest human religions, even the most unlikely story can be made into a paragon of universal worship.

Yet, for any story to become a myth, which can be effectively used to control humans, it needs to have enough room for interpretation and provide an infinite number of ways to be used to support just about any event or circumstance.

Christianity does that effectively by equipping its storyline with three widely applicable claims: God loves all humans, God is almighty and God works in mysterious ways. Any event or circumstance that doesn't fit together with any of the first two can always be made compatible with the myth by means of the third – because there just is no conceivable limit to mystery.

Thus, creating a credible myth should be the least of your worries. Besides, there are enough human myths already you can use and tweak to serve your own interests. The hard part is conveying the myth to enough of the humans who are the most susceptible to it and sociable enough for the myth to spread organically. This has become a lot easier since infiltrator Zorn, going undercover as a socially awkward American college student who never managed to establish the correlation between the number of T-shirts one owns and the likelihood of voluntary mating, introduced humanity to the concept of social media. Still, it is important to understand the basics of human learning before fully engaging in controlling them.

Good and Evil

Using myth to control humans requires mastering the concepts of good and evil. Good is quite a universal notion, used in most galactic cultures as a label for things that meet general expectations of quality. If the expiration date on a canned Herculian sea panther gill has not passed yet, it should be considered good – as should a hyperdrive engine that doesn't break down the middle of a hyperspace lane.

Evil, on the other hand, is a purely human invention. It goes beyond not meeting general expectations of quality, but is rather a fixed and incurable trait of inherent and deliberate reluctance to adhere to even the lowest standards of socially acceptable behaviour. Any human myth is completely impotent unless it provides a clear demarcation between what is good and what is evil – or, rather, *who* is good and *who* is evil.

An evil human is one who treats other humans the same way regular humans treat other animals and insects. This includes hunting others for sport, keeping others caged and fed the same cheap fuel every day, cross-breeding captive specimens to evolve new races with life threatening physiological abnormalities and cold-bloodedly murdering anyone who is annoyingly attracted to one's desert. A good human, on the other hand, is one who positively discriminates humans against other species, while systematically advancing the interests of others at her or his own expense. Essentially, being good is a human term for being a xeno-phobic masochist.

Oddly, almost all humans consider themselves to be on the good side – even if they treat all species equally most of the time. (With humans there always have to be two sides, with no grey zone in between.) Even those considered evil are never completely indiscriminate towards all living things. This is the primary reason why we always operate under stealth. If humans had known about us and our non-discrimination policy of treating all terrestrials equally badly, they would likely have labelled us the greatest evil they know. For the sake of universal safety, we would much rather have them fighting each other than pondering ways to deter an alien invasion and then accidentally inventing a black hole generator that devours star systems and has no "undo" button.

THE BASICS OF MIND CONTROL

Each human is only able to absorb a certain amount of information during a regular day. A terrestrial day consists of twenty-four hours, of which at least six the human spends on hibernation, at least eight labouring on something entirely intellectually unrewarding for the mere sake of monetary compensation, at least three hours on fuelling and preparing fuel, two hours on logistics, another two on verbal confrontations with family members regarding their disproportionate contributions to the well-being of their domestic unit, and at least one hour is spent playing online games on a hand-held device while pretending to be depositing humanium in a designated facility.

Whether to use the few occasionally remaining hours for acquiring new knowledge is at each human's own discretion – and most humans usually use their discretion for other purposes. Should the human choose to consume information during this limited time, they will most likely prefer this acquisition to be pleasurable – because none of the other activities they have engaged in during the day has been (apart, possibly, from the deliberately extended humanium deposition) and, although it seldom looks like it, humans do prefer to have at least some pleasure occasionally present in their lives.

Most humans are not thrilled by the prospect of

spending the pathetically little time they have left on having their views put into perspective or on hearing their ideological adversary make a case for their point of view. This kind of information humans seldom find pleasurable. They would celebrate the prospect of acquiring it no more than the prospect of investing that last pathetic little shard of their precious time into trying to learn a new chromosome composition by heart.

Unlike useful information, information that *is* pleasurable to a human is the kind of information that is easy to digest, that improves the human's assessment of themselves (preferably at the expense of the misery of others) and, most importantly, that supports beliefs and convictions the human holds dear (but never actually practices).

An example of a piece of information a human might find pleasurable is "German scientists just found that drinking at least seven pints of beer a day is good for your heart." Or "The neighbour's Tesla ran out of power due to cold weather in the middle of a one lane car bridge, just like you said it would. So good that you used all your family savings to buy that old 400 horsepower diesel Chevy. You are such a good human!" or "The true cause of your misery is not your personal failure to fully utilise your talents and follow your dream, but the paedophile alien conspiracy that has infiltrated the government, rigs elections and tries to exterminate humanity by legalising abortion and spreading homosexuality genes through vaccine shots."

(The "paedophile" part is just a prefix humans attach to anything they dislike. The rest is, of course, perfectly true.)

If you can provide enough information of the afore-mentioned sort to fill the little daily window of a human's information intake, you can ensure that nothing else even makes its way into this creature's knowledge banks. If you make the information pleasurable enough, the human will not ever even bother searching for other information, but will gratefully absorb more of whatever you are offering.

In the past, we used to have to infiltrate newsrooms and editorial offices in order to ensure that the right kind of myth was broadcasted to as many humans as possible, but we were not able to tailor the broadcasts to perfectly fit the interests of each individual human. As a result, most humans ended up aware of more perspectives on reality than we were comfortable with. Today, all we need to do is hack the social media and video streaming algorithms, which is a reasonably easy thing to do given how predictable these algorithms are in being completely obsessed with never letting go of the human's attention. This allows us to filter information in a manner that perfectly suits the preferences of every individual human, fashioning the ideal version of the necessary myth for everyone.

Experiments have shown that by doing so you can produce humans who know a great deal about one subject, such as the entire history of humans placing inflated spherical objects within the boundaries of a metallic frame, but be completely oblivious when it comes to just about everything else in the entire universe. The results of these experiments were so astonishing that our researchers insisted on repeating them over a billion times just to be sure, which has led to a very substantial share of the current human population adhering to the aforementioned characteristic.

Should a human, despite all of the above, exhibit resistance to your narrative – just create the impression that everyone else believes in it. Humans are herd animals, which means that they are more likely to follow the herd than to follow common sense. Unlike what is frequently believed, it is these simple tactics that comprise the most effective toolset for human mind control.

∾

CONTROLLING TIME AND ATTENTION

Once the humans have absorbed the myth you have been feeding them, it is important to make sure that they stick to it. For the most part, they will anyway. Our observations have shown that however reluctant humans may have been to accept a new belief, once they do – they become zealous defenders of it and begin displaying genuine contempt to anyone who (like themselves a day ago) does not share it.

Under some circumstances, however, humans may begin to doubt their beliefs. Such circumstances may arise when the human suddenly begins to actually think for themselves – or begins to listen to someone else who does. To prevent this from happening, there are two levers you can control: time and attention.

Time is a notion humans have invented based on the rather ridiculous idea that between any two events that do not occur simultaneously, something else passes. This something cannot be seen, touched or even merely understood, because it doesn't really exist. It is nothing and does nothing. Still, humans have invented a way of measuring it, and now time completely controls every human's life.

The most vivid manifestation of time is the clock. Clocks are special devices designed to measure every instant of a human life in minutes, sixty of which comprise an hour, twenty-four of which comprise a day, seven of which make a week, fifty-two or so (yes, it's not entirely consistent) of which form a year. We are not sure why humans have chosen to measure something in five different scales at the same time. Like with most lingering human inefficiencies, the purpose was likely to create more jobs.

Everywhere in human society there are clocks. They have clocks on walls. They have clocks on their computer screens. They put a clock on every tower they build. They have clocks in their vehicles. They even have clocks in their kitchen equipment. Virtually any human-made device that features an electronic display is designed to function as a clock whenever it is not being used for something else. They even wear clocks on their wrists, at which they stare so frequently that they are literally called "watches".

The illusion of time has so firmly established itself in the human mind that humans are virtually unable to imagine a world without time. Greedy as they are, humans treat time as currency, which they spend every time they do something. They believe that their whole life is a track of fixed intervals, along which they are constantly moving, and that they each of them possess a pot of time which is constantly leaking.

This is, of course, a horrifying metaphor which would bring tremendous anxiety upon any mortal creature who would think along these lines, including humans, of course.

Mortality makes time a scarce and non-replenishable resource. Each human is born with a fixed ration of it. The size of this ration is unknown, but there is a hard cap roughly twenty-five percent above the average human life expectancy which only a few specimens are lucky enough to hit.

It is impossible to buy more.

Virtually any other resource a human may possess can be bought, but not this one. In fact, when humans say that they are buying time, what they are actually doing is spending it on interest for something they have delayed and will have to do later at the same expense.

Given this intimidating constraint, you would expect a species to focus all its technological development on finding ways to free up as much of its precious and finite time as possible. With humans, that doesn't appear to be the case. Every time humans discover a way to produce something in a shorter time than before, they use that discovery to produce more while spending the same amount of time as before. In the past century, human labour productivity has increased by 150 percent, and yet humans still spend roughly forty hours every week labouring.

Instead of finding ways to free up more time, humans manage their time scarcity anxiety by engaging in what they believe is saving time, but which really is a form of manic determination to do more. Humans usually achieve this by jumping from one activity to another as quickly as possible, without pausing in between, by taking risky shortcuts and by sleeping less.

Our scientists are still puzzled by how this can be viewed as any kind of saving, as such behaviour usually puts a great strain on human health, thereby shortening the human's lifespan. This ill-conceived propensity does, however, provide us with a powerful lever, with which we can impair the human's ability to think. By encouraging time saving, efficiency, detailed planning and calendar schedules, we can effectively identify and fill any gaps between full occupation, making it impossible for humans to fit in any proper thinking.

One way this can be done on a micro level is by scheduling meetings. Invite humans with whom you interact regularly to long, frequent meetings. Invite as many participants as possible. This way additional time will be spent finding a calendar slot that fits everyone's schedule. Never bring an agenda – this often increases the length of the meeting even more. Ask the humans to prepare something for the meeting, thereby filling even more gaps in their life which they could have used for thinking.

Another way you can occupy humans is by launching new initiatives. Come up with activity ideas that are hard to reject (like preparing a surprise birthday party for your human superior) and invite volunteers to take part. You will not receive much love for doing all this, but in the end love is not what you were sent to Earth for.

Whenever a human is not consciously offering away their time, they can be compelled to do so unconsciously by having their attention drawn to something they cannot resist, which could be more or less anything that enters their sensory field at any moment. It doesn't quite matter what it is as long as it can distract the human from thinking anything meaningful. Again, this has become a lot easier since humans discovered remote communication technology.

In the past, our agents often had to spend hours hiding under human beds, inside their closets or lurking in the shadows of the vegetation that surrounds the human's habitat, waiting for the right moment to make a distracting sound or place an object in the human's vicinity that would be certain to capture their attention. Today, all you really need to do is crack the passcode of their hand-held mobile device (usually it is an easily deductible six-digit sequence, which conveniently happens to be the same sequence as their spouse's birth date and the same one the human uses for secure access across all their devices, including their bank service and home lock system) and alter the device's notifications settings. This way you can make sure that the human receives all the right notifications from sources supporting the myth frequently enough to be constantly distracted.

∾

Gaining Credibility

During his missionary days, infiltrator Zorn tried multiple approaches to spread Christianity among humans as an instrument for controlling them. He found that humans were most receptive to his teachings when these were delivered together with bread and wine. The mission was least effective when the preaching was accompanied by beating and yelling at humans for being sinners.

Not really knowing what to make of this puzzling difference, Zorn conducted a survey among his audience, where the respondents were prompted to rate various aspects of their learning experience. While most respondents seemed to enjoy eating bread and drinking wine a lot more than being publicly humiliated and beaten on the head with a large wooden stick, the most prominent difference between the most receptive and least receptive disciples was in their opinion about their tutor. Zorn's remarkably genius conclusion was that humans are most receptive to your influence if they like you.

Liking is a human concept of partially disabling critical thinking towards an object. The object of liking is usually granted the same level of credibility – or higher – as someone who has proven themselves to be extraordinarily knowledgeable and reliable. When humans like someone, they will believe almost anything that person says and justify almost anything the person does. Thus, if you master the skill of getting humans to like you, your chances of effectively controlling them will quadruple.

Fortunately – and much thanks to the hard labour of brave pioneer infiltrators like Zorn – there are a number of well-tested habits that have proven to be most effective in helping infiltrators win human affection. Here are some of them:

Habit 1: Avoid applying violence to the target. This has been tested many times in experimental torture chambers across the planet. The very few fringe cases of subjects that did exhibit signs of liking when subjected to violence were not the kind of humans you should want to be close to.

Habit 2: Apply violence to humans the target dislikes. While disliking anyone who applies violence to them, humans tend to feel quite the opposite towards anyone who applies violence to those they dislike. Most fictional human action heroes, such as Batman or Wonder Woman, are revered primarily for this very behaviour. The oldest trick in the book for winning a human's affection is to partner with someone who will beat them up and then pretend to get beaten up by you.

Habit 3: Have an average appearance.

Consider this when choosing your human host body. Human research has shown that if you take a large number of human face images, stack them on top of each other and average out all their facial characteristics – you will get the most attractive face of all. So all you need to do is abduct a large number of humans, melt them together and use your human suite generator to produce the optimal outfit.

Habit 4: Look harmless.

When you encounter a human for the first time, their eyes make a quick body scan of you that takes about ten seconds. In effect, before you have had a chance to convey your intellectual superiority and utility, their initial opinion about you is set, and it will take a lot to change it from that moment on. To get this first impression right, always ensure that you cannot be perceived as a threat. Simply leaving all your heavy weaponry at home does not suffice. Your whole appearance must be fashioned in a manner that does not trigger any associations with dangerous humans. It may not be entirely easy to know what a dangerous human looks like to an average human, as all humans look mostly harmless to us. Infiltrating the human police records and scanning the mugshots of all convicted criminals may be of help. You might also want to visit neighbourhoods humans consider dangerous and examine what people look like there. Note the most commonly recurring traits, hairstyles, manners of behaviour and speech – and make sure to never resemble any of that. Of course, not all humans in a dangerous neighbourhood are dangerous, so you may need to go there late at night and have to wait for enough humans to mug and abuse you to get a good profile sample.

Habit 5: Stretch your face. If you strain the facial muscles of your human suit so much that the skin of the face gets stretched into a hideous caricature of itself, with the eyes reduced to thin wrinkled strips and the lips so stiff that they no longer properly conceal the mouth, making some (or in some models all) of the teeth, and sometimes even that slimy and disgusting thing called a "tongue", perfectly visible to your surroundings to be appalled by, you will be producing something humans call "a smile". Much like laughter, smiling doesn't produce the desired effect in all contexts and should be avoided shortly after a human has died, or during the process of them dying.

Habit 6: Lie. Humans resent knowing the truth about most things that are important to them. You must therefore never be honest with humans about their appearance, intellectual abilities or the relative attractiveness of their spouses and children. Always lie about what you think of their pointlessly complex modifications of fuel, the design of all the cloth patches they wrap their bodies in or the bizarre things they do with their hair.

Just make sure to only lie about things they do not have the means to reveal the truth about, because one important attribute of a lie is that it is supposed to be perceived as the truth. Infiltrator Zorn was not informed about this attribute when he made his first attempts of using lying to win additional human affection. He was deeply dissatisfied with the net result of complimenting a human cook on the deliciousness of her modified fuel only moments after vomiting out the disgusting muck he had been fed. He was equally dissatisfied with the consequences of lying about the sack of fertiliser he donated to a human orphanage during a high society fundraiser dinner being a sack of gold.

If the eventual discovery of truth is impossible to rule out, at least make sure that the discovery is delayed long enough for humans to forget all about the matter, as was the case when Zorn, while working undercover as the supreme leader of one of the largest human countries, lied about the leader of a smaller country being in possession of particularly dangerous weapons. The lie became a justification for a war that lasted for eight years, leaving hundreds of thousands humans dead, millions displaced, leaving the target country shattered and torn by sectarian violence and costing the taxpayers of the invading country the equivalent of its total annual healthcare budget. Yet, by the time the war ended, few humans really remembered why it had started in the first place. By that time Zorn was long out of the office and enjoying a pleasant break at a ranch in Texas, where he could surround himself with less annoying mammals than humans while waiting for his next assignment.

Habit 7: Pretend that they are interesting.
Humans are extremely boring. Most of their social interactions are exchanges of information that have absolutely no value to anyone. They can spend hours describing current and past atmospheric conditions, telling you what they did during the weekend and expressing insincerely positive assessments about the pointless activities you will have to pretend to have wasted your weekend on, regardless of how insignificant these activities would have been in the context of the universe.

If during this session of mental torture you do what would be the most sensible thing and run off screaming, that may give them reason to dislike you. Instead, stretch your face as advised above, widen your eyes and use all your available energy to express just how fascinating the things you are hearing are. This will, of course, bring about an even greater flow of useless and dull information, but if your goal is to be liked by humans, this is something you will have to learn to endure. Just think about all the useful information you will be able to probe out of them after abduction, and you will feel better.

Habit 8: Rage at everything they hate. Having a lot in common with a human always helps them to like you, but what will make them adore you is if you are good at reaffirming their own hatred. If they got fined for breaking a rule, express how stupid you think that rule is. If they have stepped on a nail – tell them how much you hate nails and everyone who makes them. If they robbed and raped somebody – pretend to be angry about how irresponsible that person was to have worn so little fabric and carried so much money. If you know who they voted for in an election – tell them something scornful about the opposing side or share a conspiracy theory about those they voted against. Just please avoid blaming the reptilians. The poor creatures have received enough heat already.

Habit 9: Die. As was explained in the section about funerals, humans like other humans a lot more when the latter are dead. Die – and suddenly everyone will begin attributing positive qualities to you which you never actually possessed. Humans who always ignored you will say that you were a good friend, and those who hurt you the most will likely give you the most praise.

Dying does, of course, make further infiltration substantially more difficult, which is why you should abstain from practising this habit too frequently.

Habit 10: Use decimal and even numbers.

For some reason humans hate numbers that don't fit into the decimal scale and try to group all their items and pieces of information in batches of two, five or ten – or, if the initial quantity is more substantial, in numbers that are easily divided by the aforementioned numbers. If they have a list of nine items, they will go to great lengths to invent a tenth just for the symmetry of it.

∾

Sowing Dismay

All infiltrators who have ever worked on Earth know the saying: "A good human is a human who is busy being somewhere else." There are other versions of this saying among the Galactic Council members who voted in favour of the human extermination plan, but all tend to agree that humans are a lot better when kept to themselves rather than exploring space and bringing their junk food to other planets. History shows that humans are best at keeping to themselves when they are in dismay and entangled in internal strife.

Sowing dismay in human societies will therefore be one of your primary tasks. Fortunately, all the prerequisites for human dismay are already in place. Humans already speak different languages, use different currencies, and even measure the same things according to different measurement scales. The latter should, in itself, be constraining enough to prevent humans from reaching other planets, like when NASA's Mars Climate Orbiter burned down in 1999 after ten months of travel thanks to the inability of its engineers to agree on whether to use metric or imperial units when calculating its landing trajectory, but there is a lot more than that for us to work with.

Humans often differ in their opinion on how their societies should be organised. These differences are almost always derived from a few basic and never-ending conflicts of interests. One such conflict is between the interest of some humans in not sharing their possessions with others and the interest of other humans in not starving. As the latter sentiment is normally shared by a vastly larger number of humans than the number of those who have any considerable possessions to share, almost all human societies are designed in a way where everyone needs to share part of their possessions with others. Still, humans are so inefficient in redistributing their surplus of wealth that malnutrition still remains the second leading cause of human deaths after stupidity.

This imbalance could, of course, be easily resolved. A most basic calculation shows that half of all humans who starve to death every year could have survived if they had eaten the other half, while a third could have easily been spared from starvation had their parents refrained from conceiving them in the first place.

Fortunately, humans rather prefer to address such imbalances by simply sending surplus food from wealthy parts of the planet to the poor, where much of it is then seized by well-connected and well-armed entrepreneurs and resold back to the wealthy parts at a very attractive price. In order to fund such donations, wealthy human countries impose import tolls on any goods coming from the poor countries. The tolls are usually high enough to keep any goods that aren't stolen from ever being exported, thereby effectively perpetuating the imbalance between the rich and the hungry.

However appalled you may feel about this barbaric injustice, preserving such differences effectively serves our purpose of sowing dismay. Humans are remarkably talented at turning difference into conflict. Most of them cannot stand opinions other than their own being voiced without reprimands. By voicing opinions that are most polarising at well chosen moments, you can effectively instigate waves of unrest. There is a range of strongly polarising opinion scales in human societies which you can use for this.

One common polarising opinion scale is the aforementioned issue of how wealth should be distributed. Here many humans are in favour of having a strong state continuously robbing its citizens to create shared wealth, while others prefer the state to leave its citizens alone to freely rob each other until the shrewdest of them get everything.

Another common polarising opinion scale is the schism between humans who dislike the present for being too different from the past, and those who dislike the present for deviating from their vision of the future. The former are called conservatives and are known for opposing all change (except for climate change). The latter are called progressives and are champions for diversity, inclusiveness and tolerance (except with regard to conservative opinions).

There are many other scales, along which tension and conflict between large groups of humans can be instigated. Almost everything you have learned so far by reading this manual can be effectively used to divide human societies and plunge them into sectarian strife.

The question of which version of Zorn's G.O.D. terraformer story is most accurate has already proven to be a great divider. So have the different opinions on which body type best adheres to the human understanding of beauty.

Different human understandings of culture are also a great igniter – especially in the light of the long human track record of mistaking individual stupidity for cultural differences.

Humans are capable of turning against each other based on their differing attitudes towards other animals – like whether cats are better than dogs or whether minks should be mass slaughtered only to provide humans with yet another wrapper to conceal their hideous bodies with.

Reproduction – especially the lack thereof – is great conflict material.

Human communication is a smorgasbord of potential provocation. Misunderstood metaphors, misplaced sarcasm, contradictory body language and even completely well-intended profanity can start inter-human wars of epic scale.

Almost every tradition, rule or code is highly flammable if broken.

But you will get the greatest cocktail of human doom if you tamper with human identity, apply the power of myth to it, pass it through the binary prism of good and evil – and then weaponise it by appealing to human instincts.

The more basic the instinct, the greater the doom.

All of the above are easy methods of sowing dismay in human societies, which should keep the members of this hopeless species busy enough with besmirching each other to keep their eyes away from the stars and stay clear of any meaningful attempts to save their planet. But if you manage to trigger their taste for winning – you will really hit the jackpot.

As history has proven many times before, a human will lose everything for the sake of winning.

Zorn search party telepathic intercom transmission excerpt 9

Transmitted 6 hours and 43 minutes after the second dispatch. The human speech has been converted into readable telepathic signals for better understanding.

Detective: Humania Womanson... Is that your real name?

Gee: Yes.

Detective: Well, Miss Womanson, would you like to tell me what you were doin' tossin' people 'round in Disneyland together with that shaven monkey of yours?

Gee: The same thing all humans do in Disneyland.

Detective: And what's that?

Gee: You are a human. You should know.

Detective: And aren't you?

Gee: Of course I am.

Detective: Then I am darn curious to hear your take on the matter. What do humans do in Disneyland?

Gee: They... We train infiltrators.

Detective: Really? Is that what you were doin' there?

Gee: We were just passing through...

Balbooza: [*Gee, do you copy?*]

Gee: [*Yes, Balbooza, where are you?*]

Balbooza: [*I am back at the zoo. They put me back in that cage with all the hairy... whatever they all were. Took my trousers too. Will be harder to find Zorn without them. Where are you?*]

Gee: [*I am not sure...*]

Detective: And by "training infiltrators", do you mean throwin' folks' kids 'round and draggin' park workers into a haunted house by force?

Gee: The human wearing the Mickey Mouse costume is a friend of ours. He was urgently needed in the mentioned facility and the human offspring surrounding him had to be promptly removed in order to enable his progression. The degree of violence applied was minimal and the number of fatalities is zero.

Detective: Well, it so happens that this friend of yours intends to press charges against you. You see, Mr Zeltzner is a fragile individual, who's been diagnosed with multiple conditions, such as anxiety disorder, sociophobia, achluophobia, having-skeletons-jump-at-you-phobia and some other weird crap I've no idea what it's called and I don't frankly give a damn. He does what he does for a livin' 'cause wearin' that Mickey Mouse suit all day helps him handle his anxiety and fear of exposure to other people... Or some-thin'. Ah, who am I kiddin'... He's a freakin' furry. Wouldn't let the sick bastard anywhere near my kids, if you ask me. So, between us, I do see the fun in you giving that sicko a bit of a tumblin'. But, now this fair gentleman feels he's been – newsflash – harassed and abused by your little stunt back at the park, and as a guardian of law I am obliged to bring you in for testi-mony. The bad news is that you couldn't have picked a spot with more spotlight than the middle of Disneyland for your little draggin' and droppin'. Plenty of eye witnesses. With cameras. So don't even try to twist your story. The persecutor has it all documented from all possible angles. But, if you can get your motives right, you may still have a chance to get out of this one lightly. So, I want you to think this one through before you answer me. We know what you did. Why did you do it?

Gee: It was a matter of high galactic importance.

Detective: Oh, come on! Lose the act, will you! I'm on your side here. What did the bastard do? Did he fondle a kid? Did he pull out his wiener? Be honest with me and we can make this go away, OK?

Gee: This is a waste of time. [*Dispatcher, I regret to admit that we have been pursuing the wrong lead. Requesting teleportation beam to... Wait, what?*]

Balbooza: [*Gee, is something wrong?*]

Gee: [**Inaudible extraterrestrial telepathic grunt**]

Detective: Lady, are you hearin' what I'm tellin' ya?

Balbooza: [*Come on, Gee, tell me what's going on! Have they found Zorn?*]

Gee: [*Yes.*]

Detective: Miss Womanson, I am giving you a fair opportunity here...

Balbooza: [*Well, that is splendid news! Where was he?*]

Gee: [*Balbooza, you have been on Earth for a while now. You have scanned some human brains, analysed their language...*]

Balbooza: [*Well, yes. Why?*]

Detective: ...come clean with me and I'll help you out. But if you choose to keep your mouth shut...

Gee: [*What is that expression humans use when they feel astonished or extremely annoyed, that refers to a female they hold sacred...*]

Balbooza: [*Holy Moly?*]

Detective: ...and I won't be able to soften what's comin'.

Gee: [*No, I think it involves a sacred female engaging in parenting...*]

Balbooza: [*Holy Cow?*]

Dispatcher: [*Agent Gee, we were able to identify your location. Teleportation beam coming in.*]

Detective: What the hell...

Gee: [*No, not that. Parenting and procreation.*]

Detective: Holy fucking mother of Jesus!!!

Gee: *Yes, thank you, detective, that's the one.*

Epilogue

The Discovery of Zorn

You have now made it to the end of almost everything that is of any substantial interest about the human species. Rest assured that the roughly seven milliseconds of your eternal life, which you have devoted to absorbing the contents of this handbook with your ionic receptors before venturing off on your terrestrial infiltration mission, were a sound investment. Eternity can be a lot less pleasurable when having to live with mental trauma originating from human encounters conducted without proper preparation and training.

Your mission is still a difficult and perilous one, but at least you now know how to properly use a human body, how to imitate human instincts, communicate with humans in a non-compromising way, how to conform to their ways and how to use their belief systems to control human behaviour.

None of this first class knowledge would have been available today if not for the brave and devoted field work of the great pioneer infiltrator Zorn, whom we were once so close to losing in the whirlpool of his hazardous mission environment, but who had finally succeeded in getting himself found – despite the dreadful incompetence of the agents who were sent to retrieve him.

Having made it this far, you are probably anxious to know what really happened to the legendary infiltrator and how he was found. Well, then, let us not stoke your curiosity any longer!

Due to an unfortunate miscalculation of Zorn's inception coordinates by an otherwise talented young teleportation beam operator, who had that very year won seventh place in the prestigious Galactic Equal Opportunity Precision Beaming Contest for Youth with Seeing Disabilities, the great infiltrator was mistakenly injected into the body of a captive chimpanzee.

Having had plentiful experience with similar circumstances while locked up in a circus for twenty-four years, Zorn had devised a masterful escape from Belfast Zoo and had even managed to equip himself with some human apparel in order to make himself less distinguishable from surrounding primates. In the process of acquiring the apparel Zorn accidentally triggered a by-standing human's epileptic seizure, which unfortunately provoked a series of actions which drew some unnecessary human attention. To his great misfortune, Zorn was soon seized by the zookeepers and was sedated before he managed to signal the mothership.

When the sedative began to wear off, Zorn found himself locked up in the same monkey cage again. Realising at last that he would need a real human host body in order to get any work done on this mission, he began scanning his surroundings for a human body he could jump to by using his remaining body infiltration energy surge. He only had enough energy for a short jump.

Although the sedative was still blurring his vision, Zorn was soon able to distinguish what appeared to be Andy Ried, the American football coach for the Arkansas City Chefs.

It was only after making the jump that Zorn realised two fatal mistakes he had made. One was that he had accidentally left his transponder chip in the chimpanzee body, thereby losing all telepathic contact with the mothership or with any other extraterrestrial whom he might encounter while on Earth.

The other mistake was that what Zorn thought was a famous American football coach splashing around in a pool of mud was, in fact, a walrus.

With no teleportation energy left and no transponder, Zorn found himself confined inside the body of an imprisoned walrus with no means of communicating with the outside world. This posed multiple obstacles to his mission and research, but he had confidence that mission command would shortly send someone to his aid.

Zorn was relieved to see agent Gee get beamed down into the host body of a marine biologist who was just about to insert some intimidatingly looking object into his rectum. To the famous infiltrator's great disappointment, agent Gee seemed completely preoccupied with telling off another agent through her transponder and showed absolutely no interest in trying to make contact with Zorn, however close he moved to her. To further his great annoyance, agent Gee promptly left the premises at a pace he could not match while wearing the body of a walrus.

Zorn was again relieved to see Gee re-enter the cage later – this time together with the chimpanzee whose body the great infiltrator had recently worn. He took it as a positive sign, finding no better explanation to this return visit than Gee having spotted the connection between the walrus and the chimpanzee. Her further actions dispersed his optimism.

Fortunately, as Gee was leaving the cage for the second time, hauling along with her a very roughed up monkey who clearly had not enjoyed being rubbed against a walrus tusk in a very poor shaving attempt, she did not shut the gate behind her.

By using his whiskers as antennae, Zorn managed to pick up parts of Gee and Balbooza's telepathic communication. He soon learned where they were going and resolved to follow them, knowing that they were his best chance of getting near a teleportation beam. Rather quickly the great infiltrator learned that travelling from Northern Ireland to California is a lot more complicated if you are a walrus than if you are a human.

In his chronicles, Zorn concluded that the only real upside with walrus bodies is that they are quite suitable for swimming. He also advised his readers to never try to use a walrus body as a means of crossing the Atlantic ocean. Although discrete and incomparably cheap, this particular body shape seems to inspire a tremendous amount of biting from a wide variety of marine fauna. Zorn's brief but thoroughly unamiable encounter with a pod of killer whales along the coast of one of the Azorean islands proved that even the most intelligent terrestrial species may require a great deal of convincing before choosing an intellectually stimulating conversation over a nice good bite on a walrus' hindquarters.

Zorn's other important insight was that, although Earth is quite tiny compared to most inhabited planets and although a walrus body is a lot better streamlined for aquatic travel than that of a human, crossing an ocean in one takes exhaustingly long. The whole endeavour of reaching Disneyland while Gee and Balbooza were still there would have been a lost cause, had the same beam operator who had accidentally beamed Zorn into the body of a chimpanzee not been on shift again that day.

The time it took to extract agent Balbooza from one of the less explored craters of Earth's only moon, provide him with sufficient psychological aid and a nice cup of hot Plutonian four-eyed chicken soup before finally accurately beaming him to Disneyland was roughly the time it took Zorn to struggle his way across the Atlantic and through the dry lands of North America right to the point of his destination.

The latter part of his trip provided additional insights into the shortcomings of the walrus body as a means of long-distance travel on dry land. The rocky desert landscapes of Arizona proved particularly ill-fitted for this body type, and served as a great inspiration to Zorn's recently published two-volume self-help title *If You Hate Your Body – Try This One*, which quickly became an intergalactic bestseller.

His progress improved greatly as soon as he was able to use the supreme persuasion potential of his host body mass to provide himself with a red sport cap and an American football jersey of a size not easily obtained anywhere else on Earth, but widely available along the American Mid-South and perfectly fit for the afore-mentioned body mass.

With that equipment in place, it took less than five minutes before the first pickup truck pulled over at the side of the hot desert road the great infiltrator was heaving himself along with his four much exhausted flippers. The driver was noticeably eager to offer the famous American football coach a ride, during most of which Zorn had to endure the oblivious human's seem-ingly infinite recollections of various supposedly remarkable humans overcoming immense obstacles only to position an oddly shaped object in a desired area of a large well-mowed lawn. Zorn noted that the human's complete devotion to this particular subject and seeming ignorance of any other must have been the result of some first-class mind control work by a talented alien undercover agent who should be rewarded later.

With his unmatched wisdom and cunning – and a host body that bore such a striking resemblance to a famous human sports personality – the great Zorn quickly hitch-hiked his way to the human city of Los Angeles, where he had no trouble entering the territory of Disneyland through the intricate and very swimmer friendly underground tunnel system humans use to store their collective deposits of humanium. Heaving himself up and out of this tunnel labyrinth consumed the remnants of the legendary infiltrator's walrus body energy, but in his infinite wisdom Zorn somehow knew that he was now very close to the resolution of his lingering misfortune.

A more cautious tactic would have been to tread slowly and pick the right time and spot to climb up to the ground level and start discretely searching the area for signs of fellow aliens, but Zorn's courageous character allowed no further wait. Besides, the muscles of the exhausted mammal he was operating could sustain no further exercise (and the extraterrestrial mind inside it could sustain no more humanium odour.)

Zorn had to get out *now*.

When his bulky silhouette finally emerged from one of the ground hatches in the middle of Disneyland Park, the whole human crowd infesting this area suddenly stopped and turned to him in amazement and awe.

This was the moment when all Zorn's great effort of getting to this point could either be wasted entirely, or he could just happen to have heaved himself out of a hole in the ground right into his search party's spotlight after having travelled half a circle around the planet.

The odds were not in the great infiltrator's favour.

Although our predictive abilities are greatly superior to those of humans, they are not perfect. Even the most gifted forecasting professionals are only able to pinpoint certain critical milestone events with absolute certainty, but not even they ever really know when, how and in what context the milestone event will occur.

Still, such predictions have proven immensely useful in determining when a certain infiltrator agent is expected to be in a dire need of a teleportation beam to the mothership.

When Zorn was sent on his infiltration missions, the mothership's security systems were programmed with a set of trigger phrases, each of which would immediately initiate an evacuation protocol. The forecasters couldn't quite explain any of the phrases, but their psychohistorical data models have almost never failed in accurately predicting the most acute need for agent evacuation in conjunction with each trigger phrase being uttered by anyone on the target planet.

One such trigger phrase that had long been a puzzle was "Hey, look! It's Andy Ried! And he's all covered in shit!"

Zorn's safe return was much celebrated throughout the galaxy and has even been made a national holiday on several Zorniac fundamentalist planets, one of which actually launched a holy crusade on a neighbouring predominantly secular planet, the planetary government of which had repeatedly refused to adopt a new calendar where the year count began with Zorn's emergence from a sewer in Disneyland on Earth. (Humans are not the only species in the universe that believes in the existence of time.) After having been forced into submission, the secular planet had to construct numerous shrines in honour of Zorn, decorated with icons portraying a sulky walrus emerging from a hatch in the ground, surrounded by foul bipedal creatures staring at it in awe while texting their friends by means of flat hand-held electronic devices.

As for agents Gee and Balbooza, they both got dismissed from their service for grave negligence. Balbooza soon made a considerable fortune from selling the chimpanzee that had once been the host body of the great Zorn on an intergalactic auction, bought himself a small planet in the Epsilon Tauri system, 155 lightyears from Earth, where he made very little use of everything he had ever learned by doing.

Gee tried pursuing a career as a precision beamer, but did not make it through the diversity and inclusiveness filters due to her complete lack of disabilities. After years of unemployment, she was finally able to get reinstated as a human infiltrator after impressing the admission board with her skill in quickly generating genuinely sounding human names. Since her earlier cover identity as Humania Womanson was compromised by the emerging teleportation beam, which accidentally deep-fried a human law enforcement officer, on her next infiltration mission she went undercover under the new and even more authentic identity of Marilyn Manson.

While these embarrassing failures of infiltrators who came before you may feel intimidating, please remember that most of the earlier agents have had to operate without a proper manual and were largely dependent on luck and improvisation. With this comprehensive guide in your hand, your chances of not failing miserably are far larger than zero. Fear not and do not look back. Looking back is likely to make you want to turn back, and you should never turn your back on humanity, because humanity is a species of chronic backstabbers.

Remember that prolonged exposure to human culture may cause permanent damage to any sentient mind. Make sure to take regular breaks and spend some time at deep sea levels where the atmospheric pressure is too high for humans to roam about. It is also at these depths that you will have the best chance of interacting with more intelligent terrestrial species, as well as visitors from other aquatic worlds. Do not try to persuade them to smuggle you out with them. Unlike the transponders used in the days of Zorn, yours is fully traceable.

Breathe slowly and don't panic. Humanity doesn't have much time left, so it should all be over before you know it.

Good luck.

Human Glossary

Alcohol – a chemical substance humans consume when experiencing difficulties with coupling. Its effectiveness appears to be inversely linear to sexual attractiveness.

Allergy – a supposed medical condition we made up to help our infiltrators avoid human food without raising suspicion.

Caring – an inherent inability of some humans to mind their own business.

Cheers – a signal phrase intoxicated humans use to conclude a successful sound test proving that the glass they are holding isn't a hallucination.

Comedians – humans with the ability to make other humans laugh by stating the obvious.

Cuteness – the ability of certain predominantly infant mammals to distort the mimics and speech of humans to what most resembles symptoms of mental illness simply by being seen.

Debate – an emotional exchange of opinions between humans who have no intention of reaching an agreement.

Destiny – a human term for a single unit's trajectory in our Earth simulation algorithm.

Envy – an evolutionary malfunction by which humans may feel incentivised to deprive others of whatever benefit they perceive to be lacking themselves.

Fake news – a twenty-first century human term for information one does not like.

Fashion – a set of human mimicry guidelines, indicating which types of garments to wear during which decade and which people to look down upon.

Film (a.k.a. movie) – a deliberate visual fabrication of event chains that could hypothetically have taken place, but never actually have. Our research shows that almost all humans who view films are fully aware that what they are seeing isn't actually happening.

Fishing – a human ritual that primarily consists of sitting on a river bank with a stick in their hands, pretending to be awake.

Friend – someone who voluntarily subscribes to seeing a human's mood updates and processed beach photos.

Ghost – a human term for an observed teleportation or time travel glitch.

Immigrant – a human who resides in an area of Earth other than that of their origin. Also known as an *expat*, if white.

Inappropriate – an adjective for something humans do not like and wish to conceal without an express rational reason.

Love – a biochemical state of the human brain which allows humans to engage in sexual intercourse without monetary compensation.

Making a point – stressing important information, often accompanied by pointing a finger up into the sky.

Model – a dangerously undernourished human whose remarkable ability to walk in a straight line is wildly admired among the human population.

Moral dilemma – a situation where reality can no longer sustain the full variety of human social constructs on their regular binary right vs. wrong scale.

Patriotism – a strange human habit of feeling greater loyalty to people born in one's geographic proximity than to people one actually agrees with.

Playing – a socially acceptable human term for acting like an idiot.

Referendum – a method by which intelligent humans can make things that contradict common sense happen without taking any responsibility for the outcome.

Regret – a peculiar type of human mental activity entirely dedicated to analysing the possible outcome from options that are no longer available.

Rock star – a solid celestial body or a noisy human who systematically defies the human social norms of smiling and holding down one's middle finger when photographed.

Sandpit – a padded training installation where human children learn to practise politics.

Social Media – systems humans use to display the least important information about themselves to others while feeding any information that is actually useful to advertisers.

Style – a human term for high predictability.

Superstition – a human habit of adapting one's conduct to things that neither exist nor are visible (a bit like virtual reality without a VR helmet).

Tolerance – a human term for accepting and respecting diversity in all aspects of human life, except in opinions about diversity.

Virgin – a human who has never mated, except for one famous virgin called Mary, whose husband became known as the most patient and trusting human in the history of mankind.

Wizard – an old bearded man with a pointy hat who uses his supernatural powers to help humans install printers and configure wireless networks.

Work – a concept that usually involves humans performing tasks that could have been performed with greater efficiency even by the most primitive machines.

Worrying – one of the most popular human pastimes. Involves trying to imagine as many horrible outcomes of a given situation as possible.

Writer – a human who lies for (very little) money.

Acknowledgments

This work is the product of many influences, to which I extend my sincere gratitude. Here they are listed in no particular order:

First and foremost, I want to thank all the followers of the Aliens About Humans Twitter account. Your comments, likes, and retweets have helped shape the narrative of this book. Many of the observations included here were inspired by you.

I'd like to thank Elon Musk for not completely ruining Twitter before I could promote this book to its rapidly shrinking audience. Also, thank you for choosing the letter X, and not Z.

Richard Roper, my editor, who has both been a tremendous help and a tremendous joy to work with, and who helped me understand Britishness at a level I never would have been able to master on my own.

My beta readers – Andreas Weinberger, Angela Galliat, Cynthia Oostveen, Esther Peeters, Franjo Bendeich, Hossein Shahrabi, Moa Ledin, Nikolay Fomin, Svein Hopland, William Vives – and to all of those who didn't quite make it to the end before the window closed: I'm sorry you had to wait this long for the final version. Perhaps I shouldn't have taken your input so seriously.

Billy and Wyatt, whoever of you is real, thank you for your relentless encouragement and tireless contributions.

Neil Williams, thank you for the most cryptic feedback I have ever encountered.

My beloved wife, Emelie, for being my first reader and biggest supporter.

My dad for being my second reader and telling me was perfect from the beginning. Only Lada is perfect from the beginning.

My mum for telling me off for not making the book longer and then reading it again.

My best friend Dmitry for reading the book in three days and finding it more offensive than any other reader. How the hell did we come to this...

Last but not least, I'd like to thank all of humanity for being itself. I'd say you're the best, but... Well, you've read the book.

About the Author

Michael Sender was born in Grodno, a city within the then Soviet Socialist Republic of Belorussia, now Belarus. Due to the Soviet arms trade with African military dictatorships, he spent his early childhood near an airforce base in rural Benue State, Nigeria—a rare place for white individuals at the time, and a good place to learn what being an alien feels like.

Transitioning from sub-Saharan Africa to post-Soviet Belarus proved to be an even more alienating experience for Michael, who later moved to Sweden with his mother during his teens. He graduated with a business degree from the Stockholm School of Economics and embarked on a successful managerial career in media and technology, eventually becoming the CEO of Belarus's largest online marketplace. Later, he shifted his focus towards agile coaching, organisational change, and personal productivity. Aside of that, Michael led a brief side career as a musician, composer, music producer and singer.

Michael began writing in 2015 by launching a Russian-language blog that became renowned for its incisive critiques of Russian propaganda myths. His insights into international politics have made him a recurring guest on newsrooms and radio shows. His initial foray into book writing started with a collection of satirical fables in Russian previously featured on his blog. The idea for his first full-length book was inspired by his popular Twitter account, Aliens About Humans, which humorously highlights human foibles and reached 100,000 followers in 2022.

Michael currently resides near Stockholm with his wife and two dogs.

Milton Keynes UK
Ingram Content Group UK Ltd.
UKHW012247110624
443988UK00004B/231

9 789153 103936